ROMAN SADDLEWORTH

THE HISTORY, ARCHAEOLOGY AND VISIBLE REMAINS OF THE ROMAN OCCUPATION OF AN AREA IN THE PENNINES

KEN BOOTH

Saddleworth Archaeological Trust

Published by Saddleworth Archaeological Trust
© Kenneth Booth 2001

All rights reserved. No part of this publication may be reproduced,
stored in a retrieval system, or transmitted in any form, or by any
means, electronic, mechanical, photocopying, recording or otherwise,
without the prior permission of the publisher and copyright holder.

The author has asserted the moral right to
be identified as the author of this work.

ISBN: 0-9540702-0-8

Printed by Winstonmead Print
Loughborough, Leicestershire LE11 1LE ~ Tel: 01509 213456

FOR
DONALD HAIGH
SCHOOL MASTER - SCHOLAR
MENTOR AND FRIEND

'the study of antiquity---is---sweet food for the mind'
William Camden

CONTENTS

	Preface	vi
	Introduction	vii
1	**The Setting**	1
	Location	
	Topography	
	Geology	
	Flora	
2	**Before the Romans**	4
	The Ice Age	
	The Old Stone Age	
	The Middle Stone Age	
	The New Stone Age	
	The Bronze Age	
	The Iron Age	
3	**Conquest and Occupation**	10
4	**Roman Roads**	14
	Historical Background	
	Chester to York Roman road M712	
	Melandra to Castleshaw Roman road	
	Werneth Low to Doctor Lane Head Roman road	
5	**The Roman Forts**	28
	Discovery and Exploration	
	The Flavian fort (Castleshaw 1)	
	The Trajanic fortlet (Castleshaw 2)	
6	**Outside the Forts**	55
	The Civil Settlement	
	The Bathhouse	
	The Cemetery	
	Signal Stations	
7	**The Finds**	66
	Excavations within the fort area	
	Rev. John Watson 1766	
	Ammon Wrigley 1897-1907	
	George Frederick Buckley 1897	
	Andrew and Lees 1907-1908	
	Manchester University 1957-1964	
	The Greater Manchester Archaeological Unit 1984-1988	
	Excavations within the civil settlement	
	The Greater Manchester Archaeological Unit 1994-1996	
	The Prehistoric finds from the site of the Roman forts	
	Miscellaneous Roman finds from the Saddleworth area	
8	**The Roman Coins from Saddleworth**	80
	Coins found in the Roman forts	
	Coins found outside the forts	
9	**The Tile Stamps from Castleshaw**	88
10	**The Roman Name**	91
	Glossary	96
	Bibliography	100

FIGURES

Figures

1	The location of Saddleworth	1
2	Relief and Drainage	2
3	The Vegetation of Saddleworth in Sub-boreal time	5
4	Prehistoric finds in Saddleworth	7
5	Conquest and Occupation	9
6	Roman roads in the Pennines	13
7	A page from the author's Field Survey Book	13
8	A Groma	16
9	Alignments (survey lines) and the course of M712	18
10	The course of the Roman road through Saddleworth	19
11	Roman road excavation sections	22
12	Percival's plan of 1751	28
13	Watson's plan c.1766	28
14	Bruton's plan of the Roman forts at Castleshaw. 1908	30
15	Conjectural plan of the northern half of the fort. 1964	34
16	Site plan showing position of trenches excavated. 1957-64	36
17	Survey of ground disturbance. (Pre 1985)	37
18	Reconstruction drawing of the fort, (Castleshaw 1)	39
19	Conjectural plan of the fort, (Castleshaw 1)	41
20	The building phases of the fort and fortlet	44
21	Conjectural plan of the fortlet, (Castleshaw 2)	47
22	Plan of the fortlet (Castleshaw 2) excavations, 1984-88	51
23	Daycroft Field. Archaeological features and deposits	56
24	The Tangs and Daycroft Field	58
25	A page from Bruton's record book, Glass melon shaped beads	66
26	A page from Bruton's record book, Grey ware pottery	68
27	A page from Bruton's record book, Decorated samian ware	69
28	A temporary barrier or gateway	70
29	The samian pottery from the 1984-88 excavations	76
30	The Roman coin finds in Saddleworth	81
31	The Roman coin from Thornlee Hall, Grotton	87
32	A Roman coin found during the 1908-09 excavations	87
33	The British Isles according to Ptolemy	92

BLACK & WHITE PLATES

Plates

1	Richborough Roman fort	11
2	The agger of the Roman road at Old Nathan's Farm	23
3	The terraceway of the Roman road at Mason Row, Doctor Head	23
4	The agger of the Roman road at New Inn Farm, High Moor	23
5	The agger of the Roman road at Hull Mill, Delph	24
6	The ditches of the Roman road approaching Millstone Edge	24
7	Adeline Clark excavating the Roman road in Oldgate Clough	25
8	The Melandra to Castleshaw Roman road near Buckton Castle	27
9	Ammon Wrigley	29
10	G.F. Buckley's excavation team in 1898	29
11	Samuel Andrew	30
12	Base of oven found in the eastern corner of the fortlet, 1908-09	31
13	The hypocaust building, 1908-09	31
14	Bruton's excavation team at the hypocaust building	32
15	The southern corner of the fortlet showing stone foundations	32
16	The internal road at the east gate of the fort, 1908-09	33
17	The water channel crossing the fortlet, 1908-09	33
18	A section through the north rampart of the fort, 1908-09	33
19	Ian Richmond	34
20	The main road through the fort (via principalis), 1957-64	35
21	Details of timber corduroy beneath rampart, 1957-64	35
22	Soak-away formed from an amphora neck, 1957-64	35
23	The Bruton spoil heaps before restoration of the fortlet, 1984-88	45
24	The Punic ditch and curvus at the south-east corner of the fortlet, 1984-88	46
25	The northern gateway of the fortlet, 1984-88	48
26	The two ditch slots, 1984-88	49
27	The post-holes and road surface at the south gate, 1984-88	49
28	The intervallum road running inside the east rampart, 1984-88	50
29	Inner and outer ditches at the north gateway, 1984-88	54
30	The main road crossing the fortlet, 1984-88	54
31	The environs of Castleshaw Roman forts, 1995	59
32	The uppers of Roman shoes and fragments of leather, 1908-09	71
33	Necks of white ware jugs found at Castleshaw fortlet, 1908-09	71
34	Potters' stamps on rims of mortaria found at Castleshaw fortlet, 1908-09	72
35	A fragment of a samian bowl, shape Drag. No. 29, 1908-09	72
36	A lead lamp-holder recovered from the pit or well, 1909	73
37	Samian ware pottery found during the 1984-88 excavations	75
38	Coarse ware pottery found during the 1984-88 excavations	77
39	The Roman coin found at Ball Grove in Uppermill	87
40	One of the stamped tiles found by Ammon Wrigley, 1897-1907	88
41	Stamped tile found by Samuel Andrew near the hypocaust in 1908	90
42	The stamped tile found during the 1984-88 excavations	90

COLOUR PLATES
(Between pages 62 - 65)

Front cover Castleshaw Roman forts and the Roman road heading east
1   The Roman road at New Inn Farm, High Moor
2   The Roman road crossing the Castleshaw valley
3   Roman road excavation at New Inn Farm, High Moor, 1973
4   Roman road excavation at Causeway Sett, Delph, 1975
5   The fortlet hypocaust building, 1984-88
6   The fortlet oven, 1984-88
7   The author's model of the fortlet in Saddleworth Museum
8   The Intaglio found in 1986

Castleshaw Roman fort, fortlet and vicus area are Scheduled Ancient Monuments and as such enjoy legal protection. The fort and fortlet were Scheduled on the 17th January 1935 and the vicus area on the 18th March 1998. The National Monument Number of the site is 30359. It is illegal to disturb the site in any way, use a metal detector there or remove possible archaeological material.

ACKNOWLEDGEMENTS

Most of this work is based on the research carried out by antiquarians and scholars who preceded me. The early writers included Percival, Watson, Wrigley, Buckley, Bruton and Richmond. More recent are the reports of Margary, Thompson, Haigh and The Greater Manchester Archaeological Unit. All have made a contribution to this book but any errors must remain the sole responsibility of the author.

For their correspondence, advice and proof reading I must thank David Chadderton, Donald Haigh, Eiluned Parry, Norman Redhead and Dr. David Shotter.

I am grateful to the following for their permission to reproduce figures and plates which appear in the text.

The Lancashire and Cheshire Antiquarian Society and Mrs. S.M. Thompson (Figures 15 and 16. Plates 20, 21 and 22).
The Manchester Museum (Figures 25, 26 and 27).
The Oldham Museum (Plates 40, 42 and coloured Plate 8).
Donald Haigh and the 712 Group (Figures 9 and 11).
Greater Manchester Archaeological Unit (Figures 17, 18, 20, 22, 29, Plate 31 and Coloured Plates 1, 2 and front cover)
Jean Barnes (Figures 1 and 2)
Norman Redhead (Figures 23 and 24)
Frank Graham (Figure 28)
Unless acknowledged otherwise, all illustrations and photographs are the copyright of Ken and Barbara Booth, 2001.

Many friends have contributed to my own research, amongst them, David Chadderton, Adeline and Edmund Clark, Peter Fox (Oldham Museum), Donald Haigh, the late Professor Barrie Jones, Dr John Prag (Manchester Museum), Norman Redhead (GMAU), Matthew Richardson (Saddleworth Museum), John Rumsby (Tolson Museum, Huddersfield), the late Alec Schofield, Dr David Shotter (Lancaster University), the late Dr Pat Stonehouse and George Taylor.

To all of the above, and to the many who have furthered my understanding of Roman history along the way, I offer my sincere thanks.

I must also thank my wife Barbara who undertook the difficult task of preparing the early photographs for publication and for the photographs of the recent excavations and finds. Above all, I must thank her for accompanying me on our numerous expeditions into the Roman world and for her tolerance and patience at the many eccentricities, which the study seems to engender.

Finally, I must thank Saddleworth Archaeological Trust and The Heritage Lottery Fund for making the publication of Roman Saddleworth possible.

PREFACE

The Roman remains at Castleshaw fascinated and intrigued the people of Saddleworth throughout the late 19th and 20th centuries. Several archaeological excavations took place on the Roman fort and fortlet during this period, culminating in the major excavation and conservation project of 1984 - 1989 carried out by the Greater Manchester Archaeological Unit. For local people, these archaeological investigations and their discoveries created a tangible link on their very doorstep, with the once mighty civilization of ancient Rome.

Our understanding of the Romans in Saddleworth is constantly being updated as each new piece of research is undertaken. The Saddleworth Archaeological Trust have taken this timely opportunity, at the beginning of the 21st century, to present a readable and highly informative account of contemporary knowledge about Roman sites and finds in the parish. Included in this publication are sections on the important Roman road which once linked Chester to York together with a summary of past excavations and finds relating to the fort, fortlet and associated settlement at Castleshaw.

The author, Ken Booth, has a great knowledge of Roman archaeology in Britain and his tremendous enthusiasm for this subject shows through in his account. I welcome the publication of this book which, with its sister volume 'Prehistoric Saddleworth', will hopefully provide the Saddleworth community with an increased appreciation and enjoyment of their rich and varied heritage.

Norman Redhead
Assistant County Archaeologist
Greater Manchester Archaeological Unit

March 2001

INTRODUCTION

The Romans did not want to come to Saddleworth. The valley bottoms were marshland and the higher ground unsuitable for growing the cereal crops required to provision a Roman army. The moorlands were bleak and inhospitable and the whole area inhabited by an intractable and pugnacious people, the Brigantes. In the ten years after the invasion of 43 AD the Brigantes were in uneasy alliance with the Romans; but when trouble broke out within the tribe, the Romans intervened. After twenty years of brief punitive expeditions, the Romans decided that wild hill tribes must be completely controlled in order to protect the civilised South East. By 77 AD, the Welsh tribes were subdued and a system of roads and forts established throughout their territory. In 78 AD, under Gnaeus Julius Agricola, the Roman army constructed a similar network of roads and forts over the troublesome West Pennines. The Chester-York Roman road via Manchester, Oldham and Leeds with forts at Castleshaw in Saddleworth and Slack near Huddersfield, is an important strand in that net. The Romans came to Saddleworth only as part of their defence policy for the Romanised South.

It is thought that the Romans abandoned Castleshaw in c120 AD, and many of the remains left behind are still visible today and open for inspection. The upstanding agger of the Roman road can be traced across the fields at Old Nathan's Farm, near where it enters Saddleworth. At New Inn Farm the agger can be followed sweeping around Thurston Clough, and in the Castleshaw valley it can be seen as one straight line heading for the Roman fort. Beyond, it is still possible to trace the line of the road, with its pronounced side ditches, climbing to the summit of Standedge. The forts occupy a spur of land, Castle Hill, which lies in the shadow of the Standedge ridge. With a little difficulty, it is possible to trace the outline of the larger earlier fort, but the work carried out on the later, smaller fortlet in the 1980s, has made it one of the finest examples of this class of Roman earthwork to visit.

This book has been written neither as a textbook nor as a guide but rather as an essay on the known history, exploration and archaeology of a Roman outpost in the Pennines. Much has been written of Saddleworth's Roman history in the past. Thomas Percival traced the route of the Roman road in 1751 and along with the Reverend John Watson discovered the Roman forts. Since then many historians, both nationally and locally known have contributed to the many writings that have been published over the years. It has been suggested for some time that all the past research and the evidence produced, should be collated and presented in one publication. Whilst most of the information summarised here has been obtained by others writing from the 18th century onwards, it has, on occasions, been given the personal interpretation of the author. It is hoped that this book will be of equal interest to the newcomer or visitor to Saddleworth as well as to the more serious student of local history.

CHAPTER ONE

The Setting

Location

On the western side of the Pennines lies Saddleworth, a parish of several villages, for many years in the West Riding of Yorkshire, but now in the administrative area of Oldham Metropolitan Borough in Greater Manchester. The district of Saddleworth lies midway between the Roman legionary fortresses of Chester (Deva) and York (Eboracum). The Chester-York Roman road (Margary number 712) passes through the northern section of the parish to the Roman fort at Castleshaw, built to guard the road as it crosses the Standedge pass on the Pennine watershed.

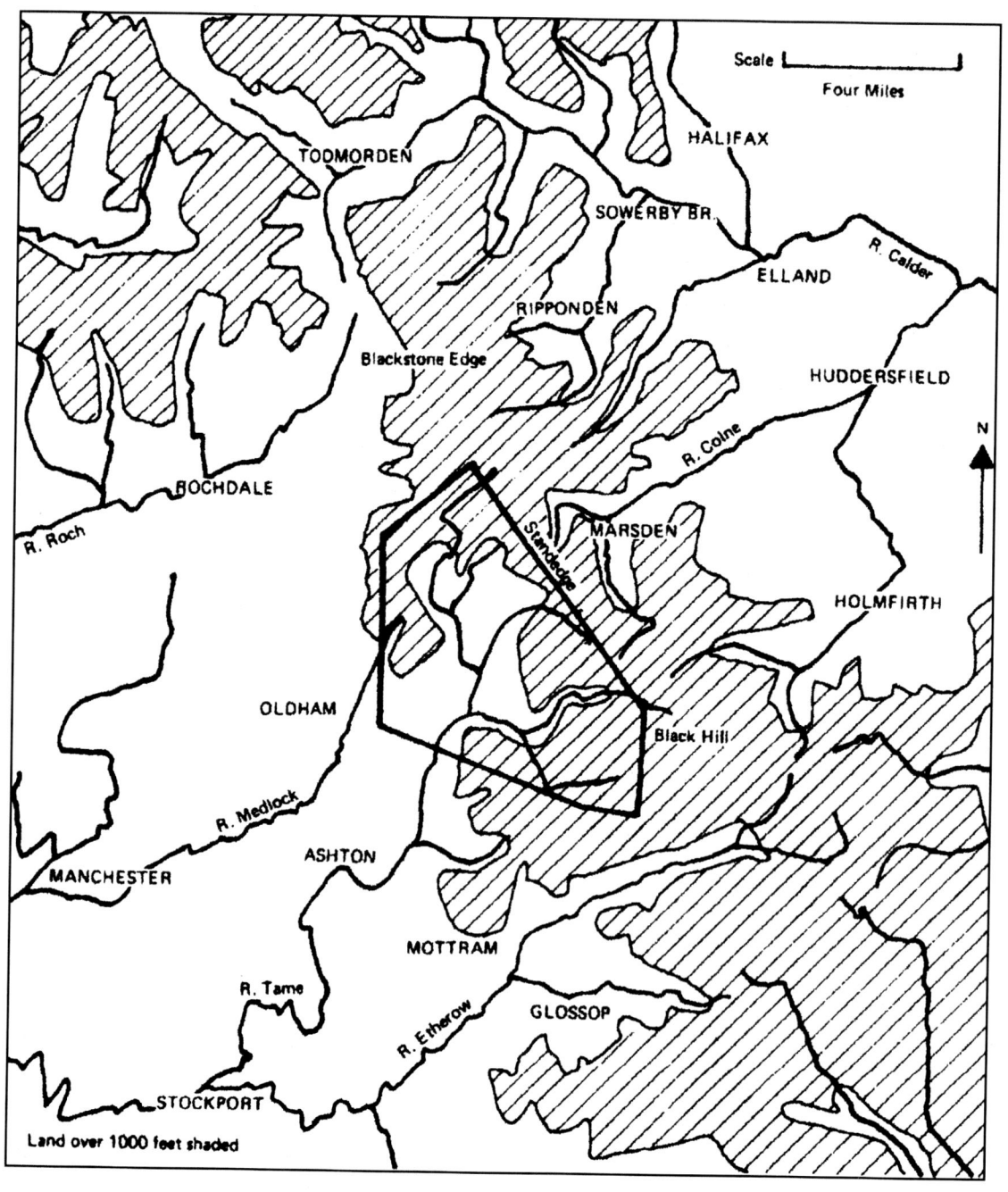

Figure 1 - The location of Saddleworth

Topography

Saddleworth is contained within the watershed of the upper River Tame and the parish forms part of the Central Pennines, lying to the west of the principal watershed at Standedge. The Pennines in the Saddleworth area are at their narrowest, the plateau being approximately 0.5 miles (0.8 km) wide at Standedge; a natural feature not ignored by the later builders of roads, canal and railway who all used this point to cross from west to east. Separating the upper Tame valley from the western plains of Greater Manchester is a long ridge starting at Crompton Edge in the north and finishing at Quick Edge in the south. On the eastern boundary of the parish, a line of bluffs (steep headlands) passes from Staley in the south, through Greenfield, where the valleys of the Chew and Greenfield Brooks breach them. The steep edges then continue northwards past Alderman's Hill, Diggle Edge and terminate at Standedge. Radiating south-west from Standedge, a high ridge passes over Broadhead Noddle and Hey Top forming a horseshoe in which, on a spur of land lying some 597 feet (182) below the summit of Standedge, the Romans constructed a fort.

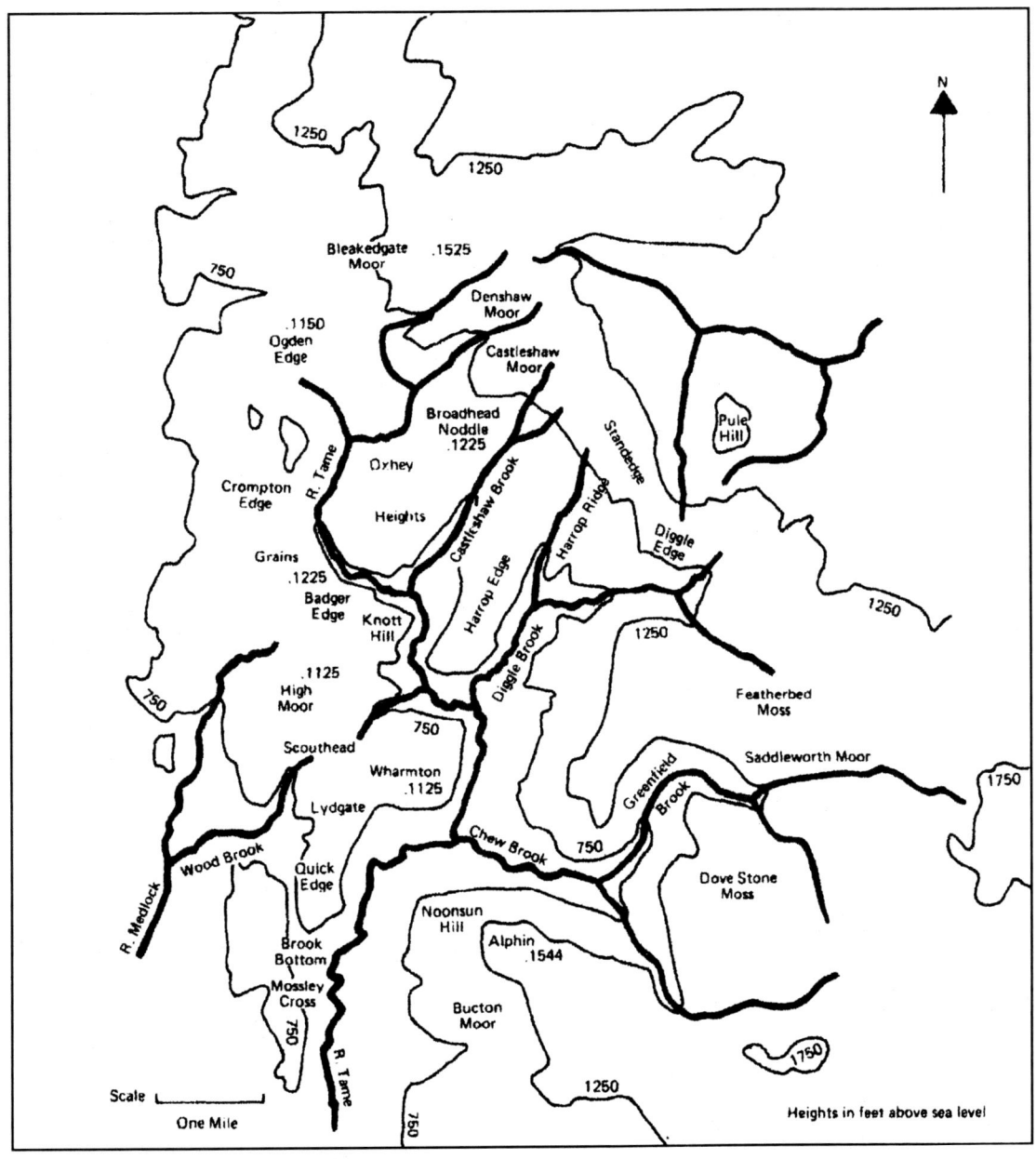

Figure 2 - Relief and Drainage

Geology

Everywhere in the Tame Valley the rocks belong to the Millstone Grit series, a carboniferous sandstone laid down four hundred million years ago. The Millstone Grit series has five subdivisions. Of these the most important in this area are the two lowest, the Kinderscout Grits and the Yoredale Series. The latter, which are the lowest, occur in the bottom of the Tame Valley where they have been exposed in streambeds. This series includes in descending order, shales, shale grits gradually merging into flaggy sandstones and lastly, dark shales. The shale grit is often pebbly but seldom as coarse or massive as those of the Kinderscout Grits. They can be traced along the crest of the Pennine anticline from Castleshaw southwards to the Greenfield Valley. In the southern part of this outcrop the rocks are much obscured by boulder clay. Another outcrop occurs between Denshaw and Delph, forming an elevated area. Above the Yoredale beds come the Kinderscout Grit series. This grit is very coarse, massive, and often conglomeratic, and forms the high hills of Harrop Edge, Diggle and the main Pennine range to the east. It is divided into two or three beds with intermediate shales, attains a thickness of 754 feet (230 m), and has been extensively quarried on both sides of the valley. This combination of alternating beds of coarse-grained sandstone and soft, quickly rotting shales, coupled with a north-easterly dip in the strata, produces the stepped effect in the upland landscapes of Saddleworth. The site of the Roman forts at Castleshaw lies on a step formed by the Grindslow Shale, a little below its junction with the Kinderscout Grit of Standedge.

Flora

Today the landscape of Saddleworth is one of gentle slopes carpeted in heather (Calluna vulgaris), bilberry (Vaccinium myrtillus) and bracken (Pteridium aquilifolium). The high moorlands are edged with gritstone outcrops and the summit plateaux covered with blanket bogs which are dominated by the white wisps of hare's-tail cotton-grass (Eriophorum vaginatum). The present climate is both harsh and wet and has produced an acid soil that is poor in nutrients, a condition that cannot be tolerated by many trees and plants, particularly in the upland areas. Tree and plant life in Saddleworth has suffered considerably during the 19th and 20th centuries from the effects of industrialisation and the pollution and pressures of man that accompanied it. The smoke from the factories in the towns that surround Saddleworth further added to the pollution of the uplands and led to a deterioration of the already acid soils. This situation further suppressed growth and created a situation where nowadays the tree population in the uplands is close to extinction. Today, as the Roman road traverses the hillsides of High Moor, Thurston Clough and Knott Hill, it can be traced crossing the upland grass and scrub. In the Castleshaw Valley, the road passes through meadows and bracken until reaching the summit ridge on Millstone Edge. After following the watershed westwards, the road turns in a northerly direction into Oldgate Clough where it is constructed in a cutting made through the peat.

In Roman times the route of the road would have passed through a more wooded or vegetated landscape. Pollen analysis indicated that woodland clearance by burning preceded the construction of the Roman road. Palaeoenvironmental evidence from the area around the Roman forts indicated initial woodland clearance followed by limited cereal cultivation. After the site was abandoned, woodland regeneration took place.

CHAPTER TWO
Before the Romans

This chapter includes a series of brief essays covering the background of the activities of early man in the Saddleworth area. There is much evidence of early occupation in the area, none more than on Castle Hill, the spur upon which the Castleshaw Roman forts are situated. Finds from the Stone, Bronze and Iron Ages have been recovered from beneath the Roman layers during the various excavations.

A detailed study of these periods of history is contained in the publication, *The Prehistory of Saddleworth and adjacent areas by W P B Stonehouse* Published by Saddleworth Archaeological Trust 2001.

The Ice Age

In approximately 12000-15000 BC a great ice-field, from the west and north-west, spread over the Irish Sea and the lowlands of Lancashire and Cheshire ascending the slopes of the Pennines to a height of 1200-1300 feet. This ice field, carrying its load of North-West drift, filled the Saddleworth valley. An irregular fringe of local drift marked the eastern limits of the field, these remains providing evidence of its course and extent. The summit plateau seems to have been an extensive ice-free area throughout the Glacial Period. The snowfield on the summit plateau would presumably leave bare areas in summer and the steep rocky slopes would harbour an arctic alpine flora. There is little evidence of the duration of this period. It is not until an improvement in the climate set in, accompanied by a richer, more varied flora that there is evidence of the flint implements that were associated with Stone Age Man.

The Old Stone Age (Palaeolithic) Period prior to 7600BC

There is no evidence of Palaeolithic man in Saddleworth. It is recorded that two sites outside the boundary have produced finds from the early Mas d'Azil period (Upper Palaeolithic). George Marsden is reported to have found a possible stone implement from this period on March Hill and in 1922-23 Francis Buckley reported a series of similar finds from Windy Hill, two miles south of Blackstone Edge. The site lay at 1000 feet (305m) and the finds of eighty flakes and twenty chert tools were discovered in the sand showing that the site was occupied prior to the peat forming. Their occurrence shows that Upper Palaeolithic man reached the area in early post-glacial times. A suggestion was made that perhaps they had been left behind by a small transitory hunting group, possibly moving from or to Cresswell Crags in Derbyshire during late glacial or early post-glacial times.

The Middle Stone Age (Mesolithic) 7600BC - 3500BC

By the Mesolithic period Saddleworth had changed considerably. Extending up the lower reaches of the River Tame, through the Greenfield valley and into Uppermill was an

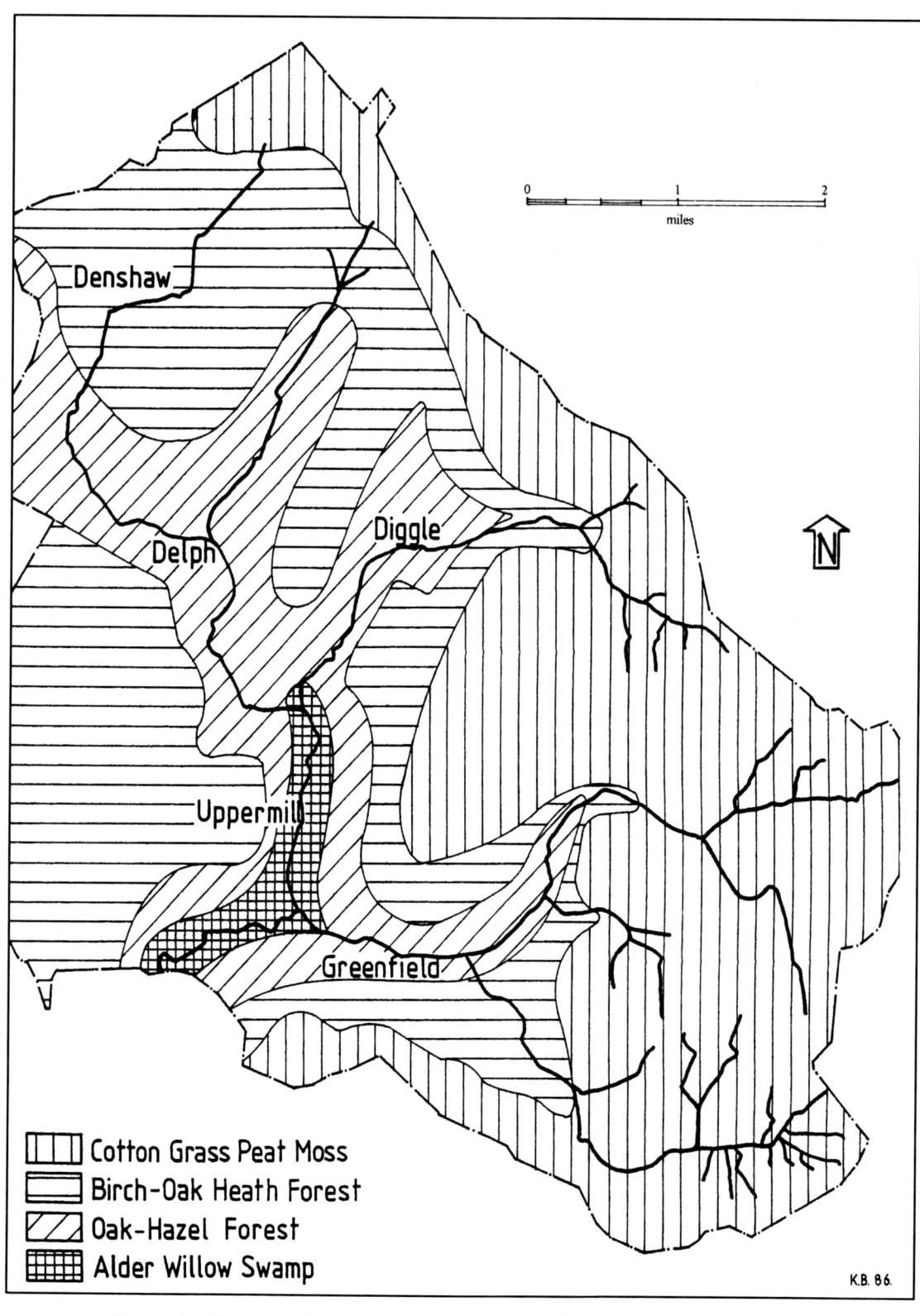

Figure 3 - The Vegetation of Saddleworth in Sub-boreal Time 3200BC-1200BC
Prehistoric clearance not indicated

alder-willow swamp and above this an oak-hazel forest. The scree-covered slopes may have had oak, pine and birch tree cover together with birch and hazel woodland on the moorland plateaux. The climate initially was warm and dry but about 6000BC, a change to much warmer and wetter weather took place. Around this time Britain became an island and some parts suffered a marine transgression, so much so that much of what is now the northern Lancashire plain was flooded.

The first Mesolithic men came on foot from Europe before the North and Irish seas had been formed. They were both hunters and gatherers, living by foraging the natural fruits and hunting the deer and wild cattle that were present in the area.

At first they moved around to follow the animals, but it is known that areas of upland forest were burned on a regular basis to encourage the growth of grass and increase open areas of browse to attract grazing animals closer to the settlements. Mesolithic man used flint to tip his hunting tools, manufacture his axes and fashion the scrapers required to prepare both the skins of hunted animals for clothing and meat for cooking. Flint (a variety of quartz) is not found in Saddleworth and was either imported in nodule form or traded as finished implements. The large number of sites where flint was converted from nodule to finished tools (workshops) found on the summit plateaus are evidence of the extensive presence of Mesolithic man in the area.

The New Stone Age (Neolithic) 3500BC - 1700BC

By the start of the Neolithic period the climate had deteriorated. There was an increase in rainfall and a lower temperature, a forerunner of our present climate. This brought about a change in the conditions of the forest floor, especially on the summit plateau. The soil, sour and deficient in mineral salts, became saturated and lacked oxygen, a state that ultimately led to the formation and accumulation of peat (vegetable matter partly decomposed in wet acid conditions in bogs and fens to form a spongy brown deposit). Neolithic man was a farmer whose economy relied on the production of food in the form of cultivated crops and domesticated animals. There is evidence of Neolithic activity in Saddleworth, flint arrowheads and, more importantly, both polished stone and flint axes from this period having been found in the area. Neolithic man generally lived a pastoral life, clearing the low fertile land of the forest and scrub by burning, to enable crops to be grown, although pollen samples suggest that there was relatively little clearance taking place in the Yorkshire Pennines. Evidence, in the form of the flint arrowheads, would suggest that movement onto the higher ground during the summer, enabled Neolithic man to continue hunting as in Mesolithic times, in addition to grazing his animals on the open scrubby woodland of the upland areas.

The Bronze Age 1700BC - 650BC

During the earlier Bronze Age, 1700BC-1300BC, the climate and vegetation remained very similar to that which prevailed during the Neolithic period. However, pollen samples taken from the peat on the moors told of a deteriorating climate about 1100BC. The transformation from flint to metal implements was not an immediate process. Rather, it was very slow and gradual. Bronze Age man was a farmer and, with the superior cutting powers of the bronze axe which he now possessed, could make ever

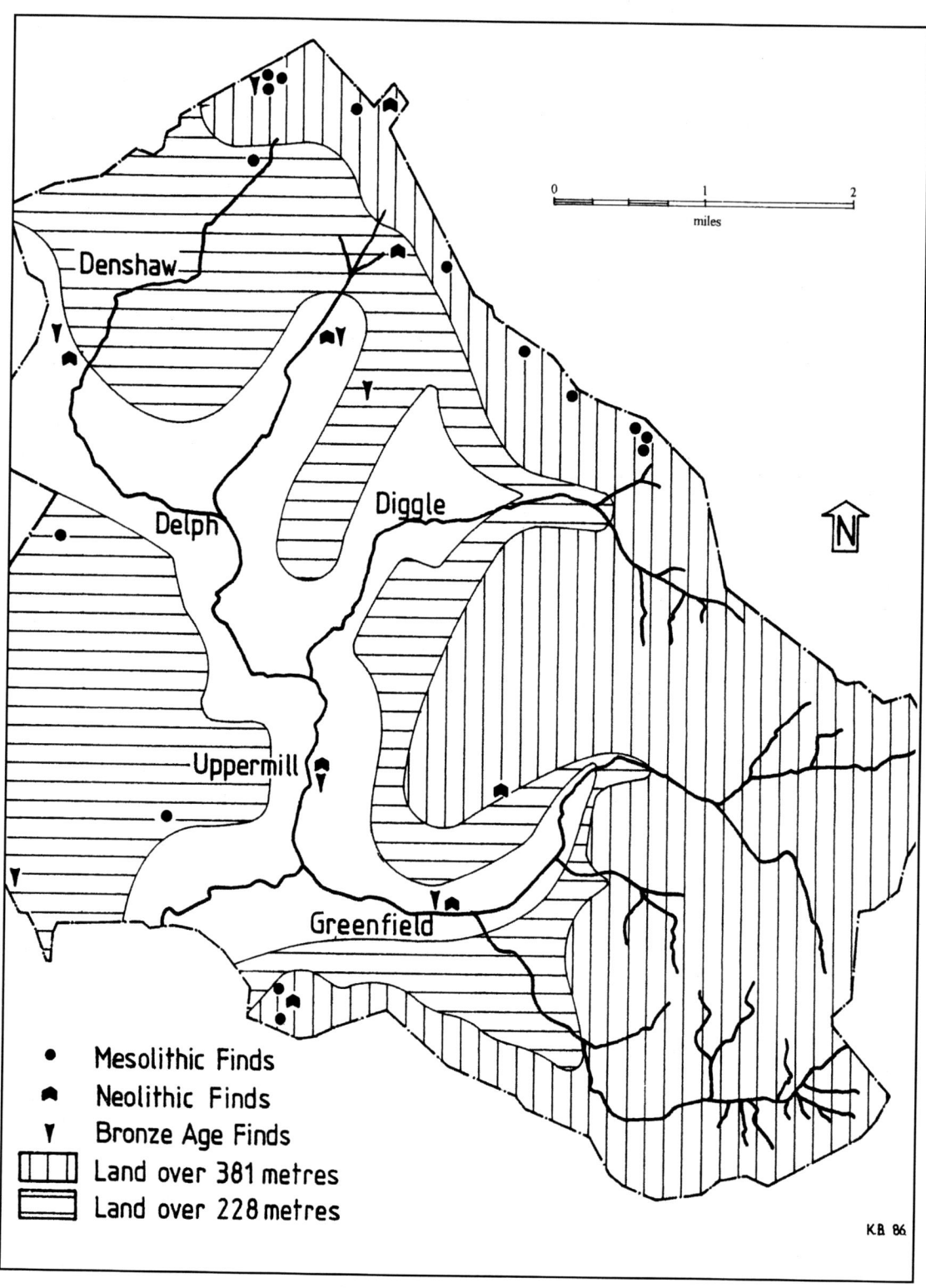

Figure 4 - Prehistoric Finds in Saddleworth

larger clearings in the forest to grow corn and keep herds of cattle. Recent pollen samples suggest widespread forest clearance in nearly all the upland areas by burning. The cleared land would be utilized for seasonal grazing of animals. The use of bronze tools gave him a great advantage over the Neolithic farmer but there is no evidence for bronze ploughshares, in fact it has been suggested that stone may have been used.

Local evidence of earlier Bronze Age activity comes from the finds of flint arrowheads, scrapers, knives and daggers, whilst the later Bronze Age has produced metal axes. Bronze Age pottery was hand made without a wheel and ornamentation consisted of straight lines arranged as chevrons, lozenges and herringbone. Pottery associated with burials is normally referred to as Beaker pottery and is usually thin walled and red in colour. During the 1964 excavations at Castleshaw Roman Fort, a pit containing the sherds of five beaker vessels was found.

A Bronze Age burial mound (barrow), situated within sight of the Roman forts, was excavated in 1974 and produced an amber V notch button together with a sherd of beaker pottery. Another barrow, scheduled as an ancient monument, lies on the top of Knott Hill near Delph and was examined by Ammon Wrigley in 1911. The first pottery in Saddleworth dates to the early Bronze Age together with evidence of the first farming communities, barrows and settlement at Castleshaw.

The Iron Age. 650BC - 43AD

The Iron Age dates from c.650BC and ended in Britain with the Roman invasion of 43AD. The late Iron Age saw more intensified woodland clearance and the creation of open heath woodland. As with the start of the Bronze Age the change over was a gradual process, and for a long time both bronze and iron was used side by side. The climate, which had deteriorated in the Later Bronze Age, remained poor throughout the earlier part of the Iron Age. After 400BC the climate began to improve and continued to do so into the Roman period. The population, which had started to increase during the Iron Age, continued to increase further. There seems to have been limited occupation on the uplands of the Central Pennines. On the western side such occupation hardly reached the 650 feet (198m) contour whilst on the drier east side it attained 1000 feet (305m).

Pollen evidence suggests that on the east side of the Pennines the forest cover was considerably reduced and a more pastoral activity was taking place, followed by the widespread cultivation of cereal crops. Farmsteads appeared and, apart from breeding cattle and sheep, evidence of ploughing and crop growing in addition to textile manufacturing has been found.

On the west side of the Pennines the story is very different, with fewer settlement sites and a scarcity of artefacts. There is evidence of considerably more permanent clearance of the slopes for grazing. Later in the Iron Age, cereal crops would be grown. Saddleworth, with the exception of a stone spindle whorl found beneath the Roman fort at Castleshaw by Ammon Wrigley in 1897, has yet to produce any evidence from the Iron Age.

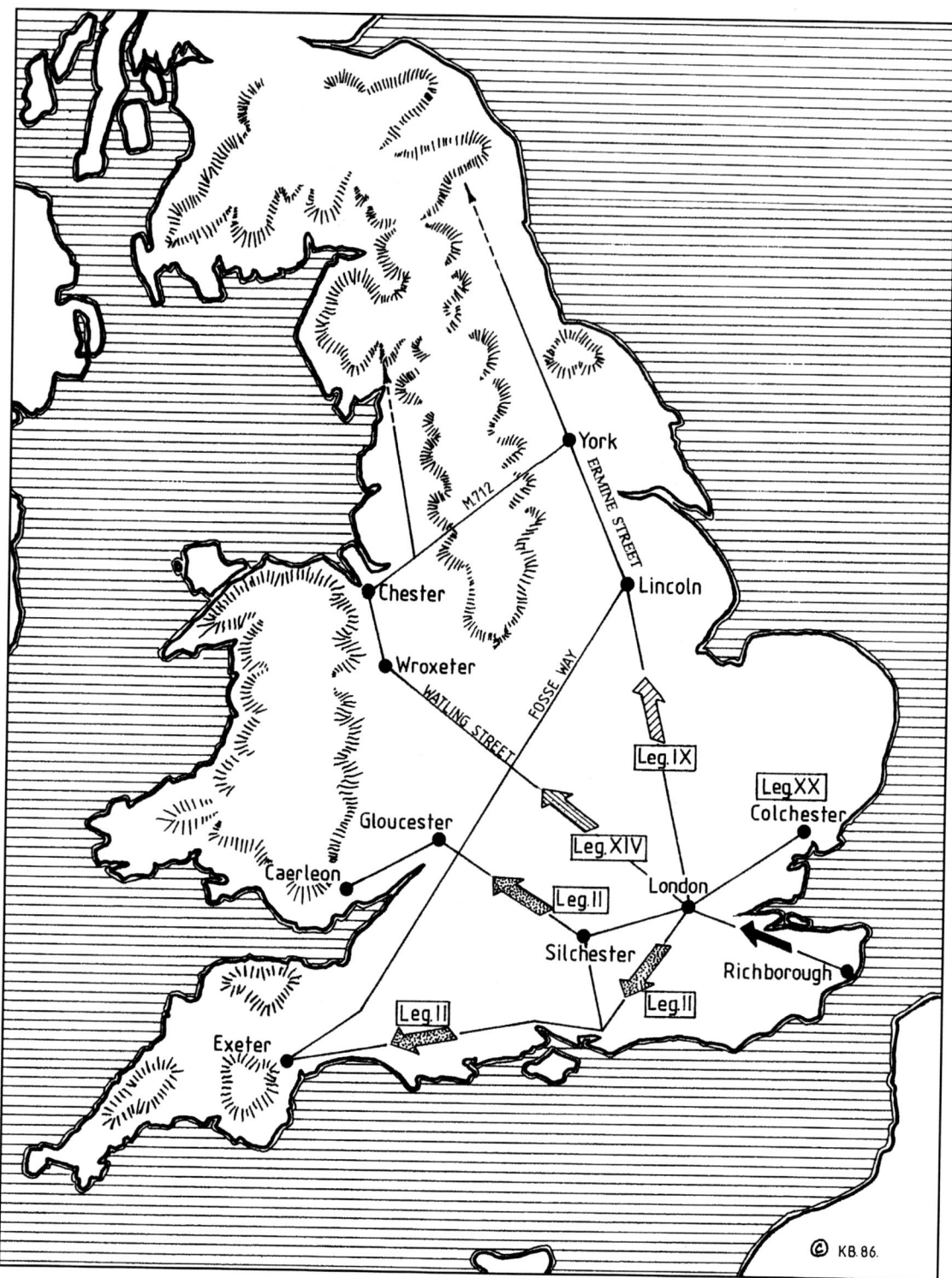

Figure 5 - Conquest and Occupation

CHAPTER THREE

Conquest and Occupation

Twenty-eight years elapsed between the landing of the Roman army at Richborough, (Rutupiae), which is now in present day Kent, and the advance into what is now Yorkshire. It may be divided into the three periods that mark the well-defined stages in the progress of the occupation of Britain.

In the spring of AD43, an army of four legions with auxiliary troops commanded by Aulus Plautius, sailed from Boulogne and landed unopposed at Richborough on the Kentish coast. The legions, which had been detached from the Rhine and Danube frontiers, were:-
Legio II Augusta,
Legio IX Hispana,
Legio XIV Gemina
Legio XX Valeria,

Each legion was approximately 5000 men strong and accompanying the legions were both auxiliary cavalry and infantry, which, together with the legions, brought the total strength of the invasion force to approximately 40,000 men.

After constructing a fortified beachhead at Richborough, which was rapidly replaced by a stores depot of considerable size, the Roman army advanced inland and defeated the British opposition on the Medway in a battle that lasted two days. On reaching the Thames they halted, according to plan, to await the arrival of the emperor Claudius who was to have the honour of leading the campaign to a victorious close. The Britons were pursued through Essex to their capital at Camulodunum (Colchester), and after a pitched battle, Claudius entered the town in triumph. This first step in the conquest of Britain had been carried out in a few weeks and, whilst at Camulodunum, Claudius received the submissions of a number of the local chiefs. The tribal settlement at Colchester was considered unsuitable for the capital city of the new province of Britannia. Claudius selected a new site on top of a hill overlooking the River Colne, and here was built a new town centred on a great temple dedicated to him. The foundations of the temple are visible today beneath the ground floor of Colchester Castle.

Secondly, came the movement into the heart of the country. Whilst Colchester was the emperor's official capital, the Romans founded another town, London, on which to place their base of operations. They had, early in the period of occupation, pinpointed London as the place from which all South-East Britain could be controlled. It was from here that they dispatched their legions, the Legio IX Hispana to the north and Legio II Augusta to the west. The Legio XIV Gemina and Legio XX Valeria were probably sent to the North-West to overrun and occupy the more inaccessible parts of the island. This stage advanced the line of the frontier to the Fosse Way (a Roman road crossing England diagonally from Axminster to Lincoln) and occupied a period of no more than six years.

The third period however, was one of consolidation and took twenty years. Soon after the Claudian invasion in AD43, the leader of the Brigantes, Queen Cartimandua, decided to ally herself to Rome. The Tribal territory of the Brigantes covered the approximate area now occupied by the five northern counties of England and included the area of present day Saddleworth. The Brigantes are assumed to be a confederation of the smaller tribes of northern England who had amalgamated in the later stages of the pre-Roman Iron Age to form a larger group. The tribal territory, ruled by Cartimandua, now acted as a buffer zone between the Roman occupied territory to the south and the more hostile tribes to the north.

This arrangement suited the Romans well and the Governor of Roman Britain, Suetonius Paulinus (AD58-61) decided it was time to strike at the source of the opposition in Wales. This was the island of Anglesey, which supplied the Welsh tribes with the sinews of war, and was also an important centre of their Druidic religion. The attack is thought to have taken place in AD59 from a temporary supply base and fort on the site of the future fortress at Chester. The Roman Governor led the Twentieth Legion along the North Wales seaboard, separating the hill peoples from the island of Anglesey. The attack on the island was swift and vicious. After the Roman cavalry had waded with their horses across the Menai Strait, they attacked the Druid population. Men, women and children were hacked to death, after which the Roman cavalry then destroyed the sacred groves on the island.

It should have been a time for celebrations but in AD61 Suetonius received news of the rebellion of Boudicea, Queen of the Iceni, a tribe that occupied much of East Anglia; he had won the mountains, but almost lost the province. The rebellion saw the destruction of the Roman towns of Colchester, St. Albans and London together with the slaughter of many of the occupants. Suetonius, only by skilful and resolute command, was able to quell this serious threat to Roman rule. The Iceni were defeated at what is now Mancetter in Warwickshire and Boudicea escaped to the land of her tribe in Norfolk. Rather than face the retribution of the Roman army, she took poison and died.

Plate 1 - Richborough Roman fort

The Roman army was now reinforced from the Rhineland and there were battle honours for both the Twentieth and Fourteenth Legions. Each received the right to include the appellation *Victrix* in their titles, hence Legio XX Valeria *Victrix* and Legio XIV Gemina *Victrix*. Suetonius now returned with his army to the subjection of the mountainous regions in the north west of the country.

In AD69 Rome's military strategy in the north experienced some difficulty. Up to that time Queen Cartimandua had remained dominant, but late in this period she divorced her consort, Venutius, and married his armour-bearer, Vellocatus. The following struggle for power resulted in the intervention by Roman troops in support of Cartimandua, who was eventually rescued and finally disappeared from history. Venutius, who now controlled Brigantia, was hostile to Rome and in AD71 the recently appointed governor, Petillius Cerialis, planned a concerted attack on the Brigantes from both the east and the west. From the fortress at Lincoln the Romans advanced across the Humber and into the Plain of York. In AD71 the campaigning Ninth Legion built winter quarters at York, only fifteen miles from Aldborough, the chief settlement of the Brigantes. Using York as their base, the Roman army began the conquest of the north, eventually culminating in the embracing of Brigantia into Roman rule. This extended the northern limit of Roman occupation to the Tyne/Solway line.

In AD74 Julius Frontinus replaced Petillius Cerialis as the governor of Roman Britain. As part of the preparations for the conquest of northern Britain, he transferred the Second Legion from Lincoln to construct a new timber legionary fortress at Chester. During this time it is thought that Frontinus probed the western flank of Brigantia. The existence of pre-Agricolan forts at Ribchester, Manchester and probably Castleshaw, substantiates this. Inscriptions found within the fortress at Chester confirm that its reconstruction in stone was in progress in AD78, the year that Frontinus was replaced as governor by Julius Agricola.

By AD79 Agricola was occupying northern Brigantia and his thoughts were to protect his army from attack from the south if he were to campaign further northwards into Scotland. In order to exercise tight military control of the Brigantes, a network of roads and forts was constructed to divide the land into manageable areas. Agricola's campaigns are well documented by his son-in-law, the historian Tacitus. His *Agricola* is a eulogistic description of the career of his father-in-law, probably the most famous of the governors of Roman Britain.

The road that Agricola constructed across the Pennines connecting the legionary fortresses of Chester and York was part of the plan to partition the Pennines.

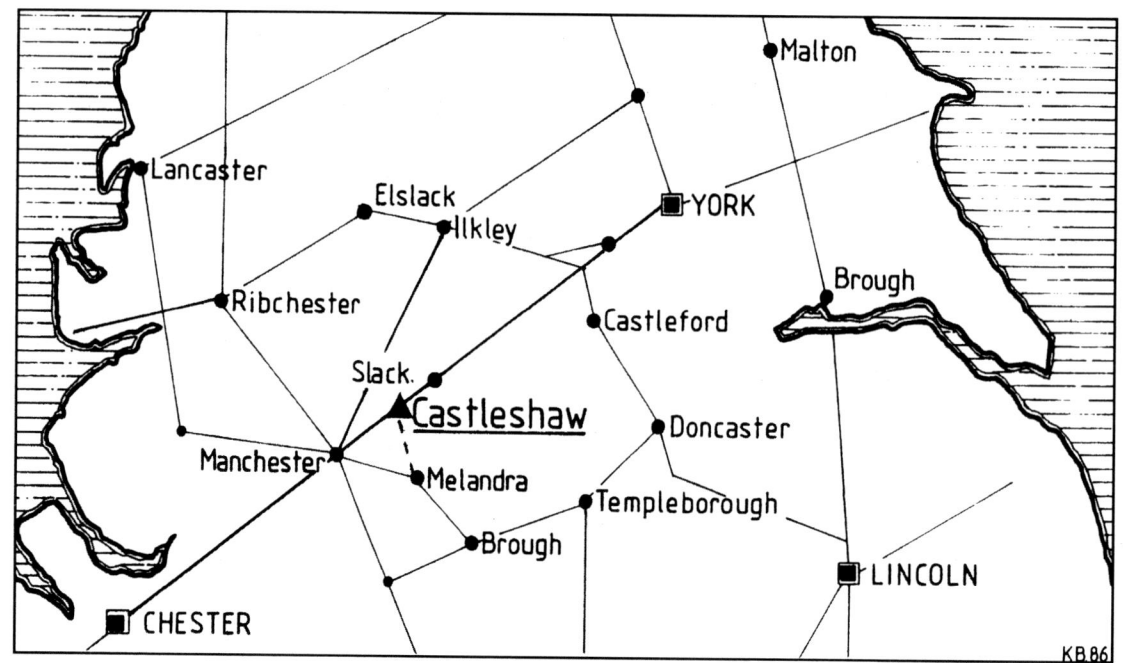

Figure 6 - Roman roads in the Pennines

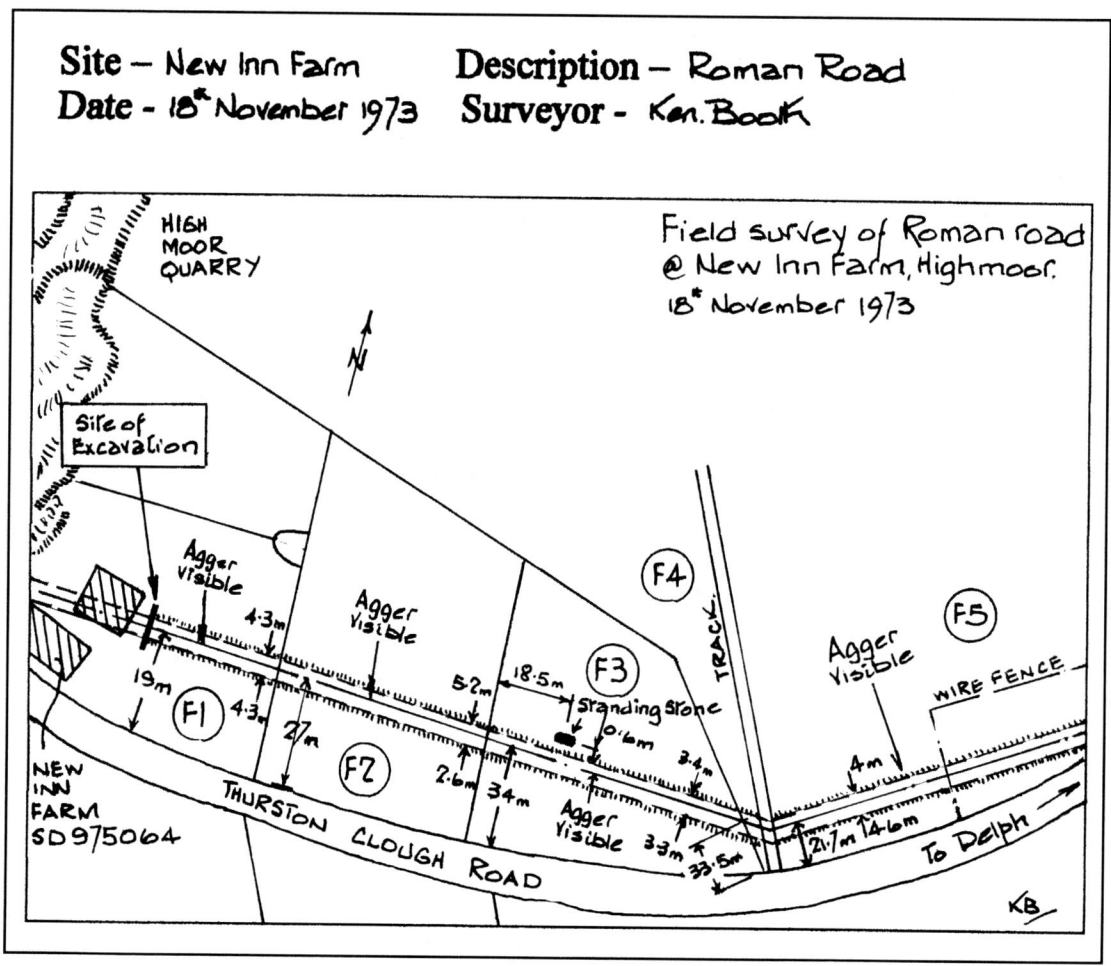

Figure 7 - A page from the author's Field Survey Book

CHAPTER FOUR
Roman Roads

The Chester to York Road M712

Historical Background

The first known description of the route of the Roman road through Saddleworth was in a paper by Thomas Percival published by the Royal Society in 1751. John Watson, in his notes of 1760 now in the Bodleian Library, followed Percival's route but added more detail in certain areas. Both men lived near Saddleworth. Thomas Percival (1719-1762), a country gentleman and antiquarian, lived in Royton, near Oldham. The Reverend John Watson (1725-1783), incumbent of Ripponden and Halifax's historian, became ultimately the rector of Stockport. It is possible that both travelled along the Roman road as it passed through Saddleworth. Percival and Watson jointly discovered the two Roman forts at Castleshaw. Later, Watson located the site of the fort at Slack, near Huddersfield, and eventually the fort at Melandra, near Glossop.

It is at this point worthwhile quoting the Saddleworth section from both papers.

Thomas Percival
It crosses hence, and is very visible in the grounds of John Mayol, of Wellihole. It then goes through the Rev. Mr Townson's land, leaving Heigh-chapel a little to the south, and so goes up the hill to Austerlands on the the upper side of the village making towards the High Moor; and going along the enclosures on the south edge of it comes close to Knothill in Saddleworth, and along the side of Knot-lane, and so crosses over the present road from Manchester to Huddersfield at Delph, and goes over the fields to Castleshaw.

At Castleshaw I was well pleased to find a double Roman camp, and on looking into Ravennas's geography to find between Mantio and Camboduno the name Alunna, which in my opinion is the name of this camp.

From Alunna or Castleshaw the Roman way goes directly for the hill called Clowze-moss, where it was cut through the moss, and is called Old Gate, being visible by the greenness of its tract; so over the top of Clows or Clowze-moss. It is visible in a green tract over the Reaps (a hill so called) leaving March-hill or Marshill a little to the north, and Marsden about a mile and a half to the south,...

John Watson
...it enters the land belonging to James Wild of New Earth and going over it crosses the road from Rochdale to Mottram at Lees Brook and proceeding directly over the land of Miles Mayal of Wellyhole it leaves Hey Chapel (otherwise called Lees Chapel) a few roods to the right, goes up the hill and crosses the road from Rochdale to Saddleworth Chapel about 200 yards to the east of the village of Austerlands. It proceeds nearly parallel with the present road from Oldham to Huddersfield but on the south thereof and crosses the said road about 100 yards above the Dissenting Meeting House at Delph, having left Knot Hill a little to the left. It then strikes over the enclosures to Castleshaw

where is the supposed Alunna (mentioned in the Ravenna's Geography) and runs parallel with the southern rampart.(it is said that coins and amber beads, pieces of pot and bricks have been found here, as also an inscription on stone which not being understood was broke and used, but there is only tradition for this). Then going directly for the hills gives a small winding turn and runs over Cloughs Moss being there called the Old Gate. It was certainly cut through the moss, 16 yards wide or more but is now grown up almost level. It is visible in a green track over the Reaps and it leaves March Hill, which is a remarkable round small capped hill about a quarter of a mile to the left. It points full on Pole Moor, alias Cupwith, alias Slaightwait Moor and may be easily seen going over that moor from the top of Cloughs Moss. From thence it goes to the Slack...

Following Percival and Watson, many later writers described the course of the road including I.D.Margary in 1957 in his classic book *Roman Roads in Britain*. His route was as follows,

At Austerlands a lane climbs steeply upwards from the Huddersfield Road to High Moor, at first very straight and, in fact, the last portion of the actual alignment begun in Manchester, then curving somewhat along the hill-side by Thurston Clough to Delph, mainly as a terraced road. Descending rather steeply into Delph, our road is then continued by a straight but narrow lane, below the main Huddersfield road, (probably the modern road to Castleshaw Camp School) to the Castleshaw Roman fort situated on a spur just to the east of the large reservoirs.
From Castleshaw the road climbed on to the moors northward to March hill, now buried in the peat, but traceable in places by slight differences in the vegetation. It seems certain, however, that from near this point the present Oldham-Huddersfield road, which runs in long straight lengths, represents it as far as Pole Moor.

At this time the accepted route from Austerlands was Thorpe Lane, Thurston Clough Road, and Knarr Barn Lane, through Delph and along the Pack Horse Road to Castleshaw.

The names or numbers, if any, that the roads bore in Roman times are not known. I.D. Margary has supplied a modern system of numbering now used by Roman road fieldworkers. The road through Saddleworth is Margary 712.

In 1970, a group of students from Saddleworth W.E.A. and Bradford Grammar School Archaeological Society formed the 'The 712 Group'. Led by Donald Haigh, a master at Bradford Grammar School, they began a programme of research into the route of the Roman road through Saddleworth and beyond. The booklet *Saddleworth Seven One Two* (now out of print) detailing their findings appeared in 1982.

Surveying the Roman Road

The Romans, having decided to construct a road connecting Chester with York, began the task of surveying the route. There were two types of Roman surveyors, the *agrimensores* who dealt strictly with the land and the *gromatici*, who were road surveyors. The *gromatica* would have been subjected to a rigorous professional training, often in the army, and were equipped with a selection of accurate instruments. The basic instrument they used to assist in the laying out of the road was the *groma*.

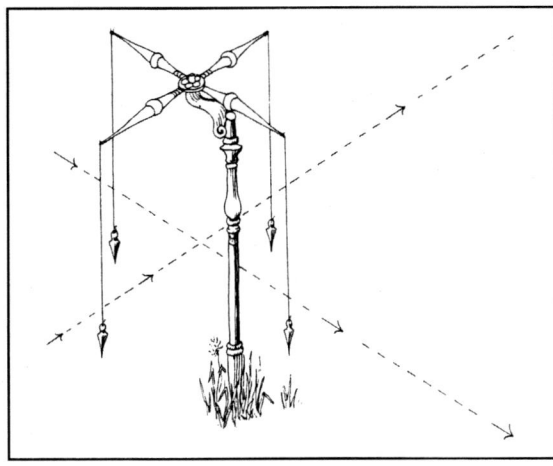

Figure - 8 A Groma

This consisted of a crossbar set horizontally at the top of a staff. From the four points of the cross, plumb lines were suspended which allowed both straight lines and right angles to be set up by eye.

Distances were measured using rods but it is known that the Romans had a machine called a 'hodometer'. This instrument caused a rounded pebble to fall into a metal bowl after each Roman mile. It was mounted on a cart with special wheels four Roman feet (1.2m) in diameter (twelve and a half Roman feet (3.7m) in circumference). For each Roman mile, the wheels revolved 400 times. The Roman surveyors had a levelling instrument, the *dioptra*, which was very similar in design to the modern Plane Table but had the ability to tilt. When used with a levelling staff, it was an essential instrument in the setting out of aqueducts and bridges. Before road construction began, the surveyors would thoroughly reconnoitre the route on foot. It was essential to identify obstacles and note both the geology and the state of the terrain before a route could be planned. The route of a Roman road, whilst attempting to follow a straight line, is more accurately made up of a number of straight lengths or alignments. Changes in direction took place at pre-planned sighting points, usually on high ground. These sighting points would be mutually visible, possibly with the aid of fires and beacons. Roman roads were not absolutely straight in this part of the country, the surveyors had to make the best use of the terrain. To descend escarpments or crossing rivers, they adopted the zigzag method. They also dug terrace ways or made cuttings rather than adhere to a straight alignment. Slight deviations to avoid natural obstacles and steep hills are known. When crossing marshland, the use of brushwood foundations beneath the road proper was not uncommon.

The construction of the road

The Romans were well aware that they could not hold a great Empire together without good roads. They were essential for the movement of troops, goods and the couriers carrying official orders and news. As a symbol of the power of Rome and the permanence of occupation, the roads of Roman Britain played a symbolic as well as a practical role.

The roads built by the Romans were the first that were based on scientific principles, with foundations, surfaces, culverts and drainage ditches. Although the correct procedure, according to historical evidence was to build up the road in a number of layers of material, it is clear that the construction of roads followed no fixed rule but varied according to the situation and materials available.

The Roman poet Statius (cAD81-96) gives an account of the making of the Via Domitiana, which ran along the coast from Sinuessa to Naples in Italy;

Here the first task is to open furrows, cutting through the old tracks; and then, digging deep, to carve a hollow. Next, when the hollow is completed, it is filled with material brought from elsewhere, preparing a foundation for the swelling body of the road. The ground must not be unstable, nor the foundation treacherous; the bedding layer must not yield to the weight of traffic. Kerbstones are set on both sides, with numerous wedge shaped stones as clamps.

Not all Roman roads were constructed to such high standards and many Pennine roads were fairly basic. When excavated, the roads crossing Saddleworth were found constructed upon the cleared surface of the ground. The road embankment, called the causeway by earlier writers is now known as the *agger* (latin). The presence of the agger is often the only remaining visible evidence of a Roman road nowadays. The agger generally varied in height and width. Sometimes it was merely beaten earth or clay, at others carefully built-up layers of stony material. The roadway itself was placed on the agger and was not necessarily as wide as the latter. The roadway sometimes had a foundation of big stones below a surface of gravel, small stones or flint and was cambered for drainage. On each side were ditches to assist with the removal of water and as a linear quarry from which to obtain construction material. In some cases, when the ditches were set well back from the edge of the road, they served the purpose of demarcating a 'road zone'. The Roman roads in Britain were by no means standardised, varying considerably in width. The aggers in Saddleworth varied from 39 feet (12m) to 19 feet (6m) in width.

The following description of the Saddleworth alignments and the route of the Roman road from Austerlands to Castleshaw is taken from *Saddleworth Seven One Two*.

The Saddleworth Alignments

In their preliminary survey, the Romans considered a straight line from Chester to York and positioned their forts along it as often as possible. Manchester and Castleshaw forts are so situated. The road linking the forts was then laid out, along the shortest possible route, according to the nature of the landscape. The route into the western Pennines, and the resulting difficulties of terrain in the Saddleworth area, caused the Roman surveyors to split the Manchester - Castleshaw stretch into two alignments, with the major sighting point being High Moor, a 1150 ft (350m) hill near Scouthead, from which the Manchester fort would be visible to the south-west and the Castleshaw fort to the north-east. The first alignment was taken from a low hill about 2 miles (3.2 km) south west of the Manchester fort (Gorse Hill, Stretford, near Old Trafford Cricket Ground) to a point on the southern side of High Moor in Saddleworth. The second alignment was made from High Moor to the south-west corner of the larger Castleshaw fort (Castleshaw 1), thereby, incidentally, proving that the forts were built before the road, and that the date of the road is similar to the Agricolan date for the fort.

The first alignment was closely followed for most of its 12 miles (c20km) as it ran through fairly easy terrain. The High Moor-Castleshaw alignment gave more problems, and was used only from the crossing of the River Tame (in Delph) to the Castleshaw fort. There were several difficulties; the Tame valley had to be crossed; the steep sided slopes of Knott Hill traversed, since the hill was too difficult to go over; Thurston Clough had to be crossed at a point above its steep sided lower course; the peat covered parts of High

Moor had to be skirted; and a constant watch was required on the steepness of the gradients.

The route of the Roman road M712 through Saddleworth

The Roman road, after passing through Oldham, enters Saddleworth at Austerlands. Along the route being described, the first visible remains, lying exactly along the first alignment, exist as two aggers, 24 feet (7m) to 35feet (11m) wide, up to 2feet (0.6m) high, each a number of yards (metres) long at Lower Thorpe Farm and near Old Nathans. Their presence disproves the views of earlier writers, including the Ordnance Survey, that Thorpe lane was the Roman road. Across the fields between Old Nathan's and Doctor Lane Head are scattered traces of gritstone metalling in walls and on the ground along the alignment, together with a low agger south of Daisy Hollow Farm. (In 1995 an excavation was carried out in this area by the University of Manchester Archaeological Unit in advance of the construction of a new haul road connecting High Moor Quarry to the nearby A62 trunk road. The Roman road was located on the alignment previously recorded by the 712 Group).

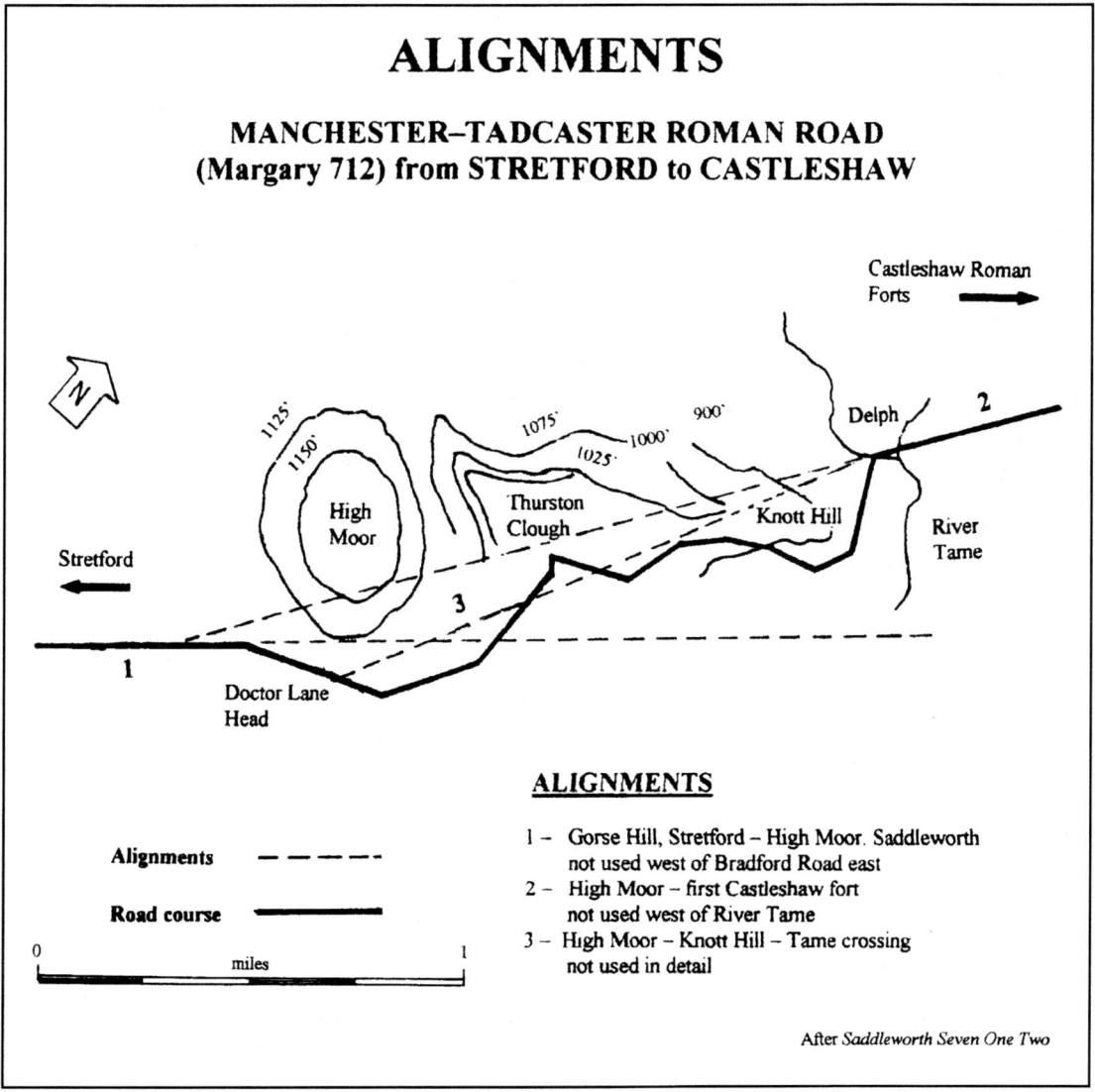

Figure 9 - Alignments (survey lines) and course of M712

The course of the ROMAN ROAD through SADDLEWORTH

═══ Roman Road – course certain

- - - - Roman Road - course inferred

0 ──────────────── ½
Scale in Miles

EXCAVATIONS ╬

A - Old Nathan's - SD963058
(Excavated by Saddleworth Historical Society 1981)

B - High Moor - SD971062
(Excavated by Greater Manchester Archaeological Unit 1995)

C - New Inn Farm - SD975064
(Excavated by The 712 Group 1973)

D - Causeway Sett - SD991087
(Excavated by The 712 Group 1975)

VISIBLE REMAINS

Old Nathan's – Long stretch of agger visible across the fields.

Doctor Lane Head – Terrace-way visible in the field opposite the 'Old Original' public house.

New Inn Farm – Agger visible across the fields descending into Thurston Clough.

Stoneswood – Agger visible at the side of the road below Stones Wood House.

Little Knott Hill – Terrace way visible skirting around the hill side.

Causeway Sett – Agger visible from corner of Hull Mill Dam across the fields to the south west corner of the Roman fort.

Coal Hill Slades – Agger visisible from just above the Roman forts to the summit of Millstone Edge.

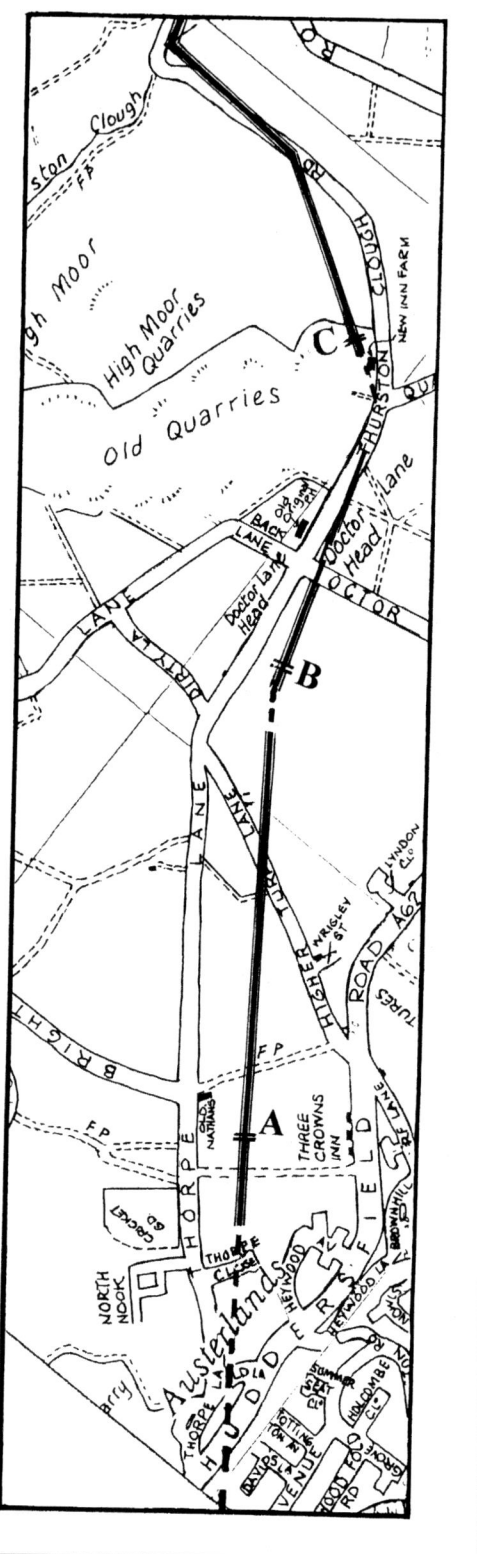

Figure 10 - The course of the Roman road

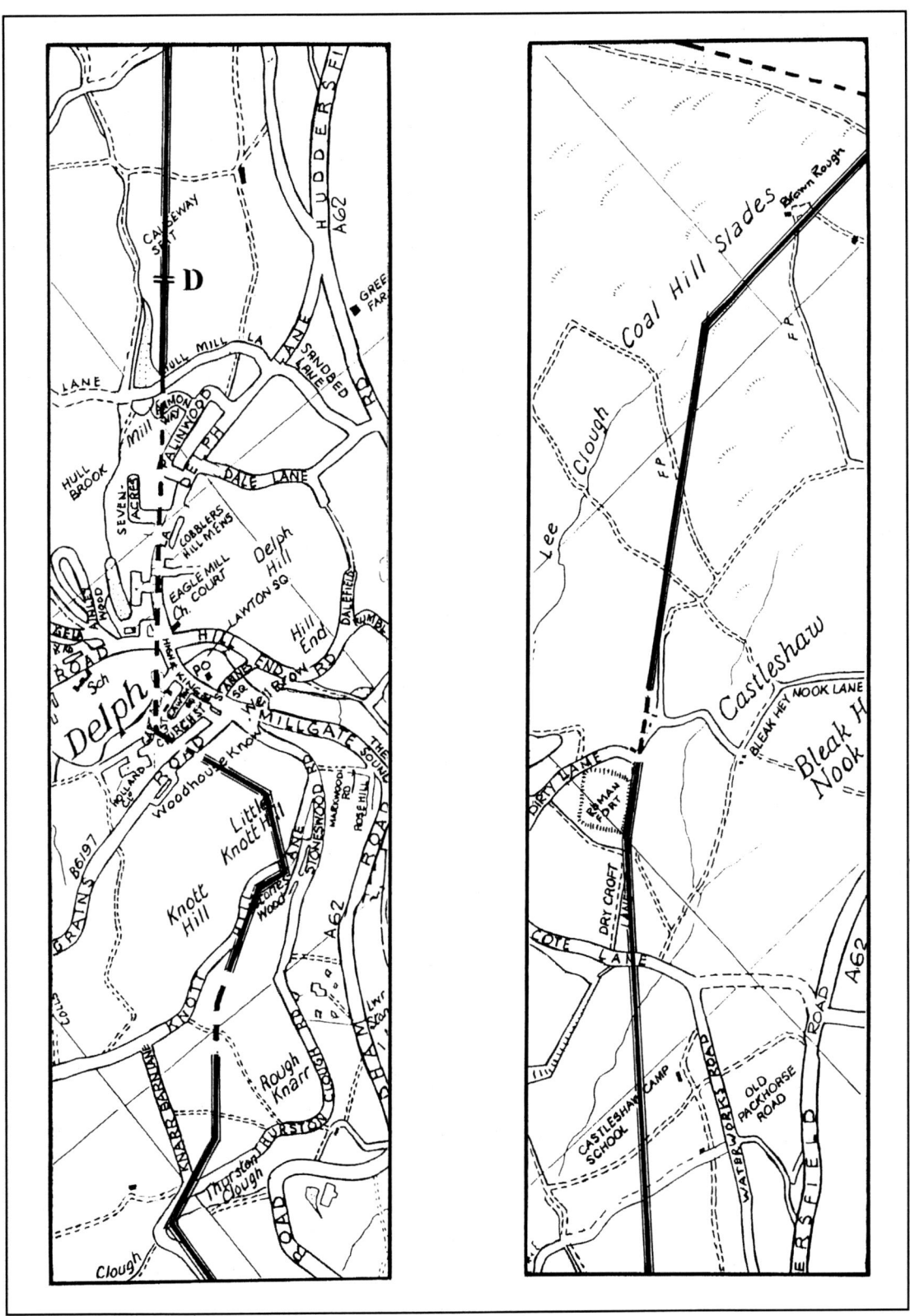

Figure 10A - The course of the Roman road

A short distance beyond Daisy Hollow Farm the first alignment ends just before the High Moor sighting point, where owing to extensive quarrying, possible traces of the Roman signal station which might well have been there, have been lost. The Roman road now changes direction three times as it sweeps around the side of High Moor to cross Thurston Clough. Along the first stretch is a piece of agger just west of Doctor House, whilst in the field opposite Mason Row there is a good stretch of terrace-way which merges into the modern Thurston Clough Road for a short distance before the Roman road appears just east of New Inn Farm, having changed its course. At New Inn Farm, in the excavated section cut in 1973, a fine agger of rammed sandstones and gravel was revealed. It was supported on the downward side by a buttress of stones from the whole of which a long tail of sand had been washed downhill. It was about 20feet (6m) wide and almost 2feet (0.6m) thick in the centre. Originally it would have been surfaced with smaller stones and gravel.

Between New Inn Farm and Higher House remains of the agger are visible in the fields north of Thurston Clough Road, both on the ground from the opposite hillside and on air photographs. At Set Stones (possibly a significant name) a curving agger 7m wide may be seen just south of the modern road as the Roman road swings round to cross Thurston Clough at a point immediately upstream of the present bridge, where however, no traces remain. The route of the Roman road from Doctor Lane thus far, is consistent with Percival's account of 1751 but not as interpreted by many subsequent writers.

A short straight alignment, initially along the northern side of the modern road, brings the Roman road out of Thurston Clough to a turn in the field south east of Knarr Barn Farm, not up Knarr Barn Lane as other writers have stated. Between the field where the turn is made and Knott Hill Lane are the remains of a slight agger, revealed by melting snow some years ago, and a terraceway as the road approaches Slack Field. South of the curving line of Knott Hill Lane, opposite Stoneswood, are the remains of a massive curving agger 34feet (10m) wide and up to 5feet (1.5m) high with the township boundary between Friarmere and Shawmere running parallel to it some 11feet (3.4m) away on the north side of Knott Hill Lane, which has clearly developed from a medieval hollow-way alongside the Roman road. The road now leaves Knott Hill Lane, contours around Knott Hill and runs down towards Delph village on a well-marked terraceway 25feet (7m) wide, which, together with the Knott Hill Lane agger, is clearly shown on air photographs.

The course of the Roman road below Grains Road is uncertain, and zigzags may have been used on the steepest portions. To return to the exact line of the High Moor - Castleshaw alignment, a crossing of the River Tame was almost certainly made several yards upstream from the present Delph Bridge at a point where the Friarmere boundary crosses the stream, near to a row of cottages at right angles to the River Tame. This is also probably the point where the medieval Saltergate crossed the stream. Numerous medieval references to the way from Standedge to Knott Hill which 'passeth the water of Tame' also refer to this point. In 1885 workmen reported the finding of a paved road when digging a drain in the vicinity but interpreted it as a road 'up the Bottoms'. It may well have been the Roman road instead. Nearby there is a ford of some antiquity, with paving stones visible in places, although it is more probable that the Roman crossing was a wooden bridge.

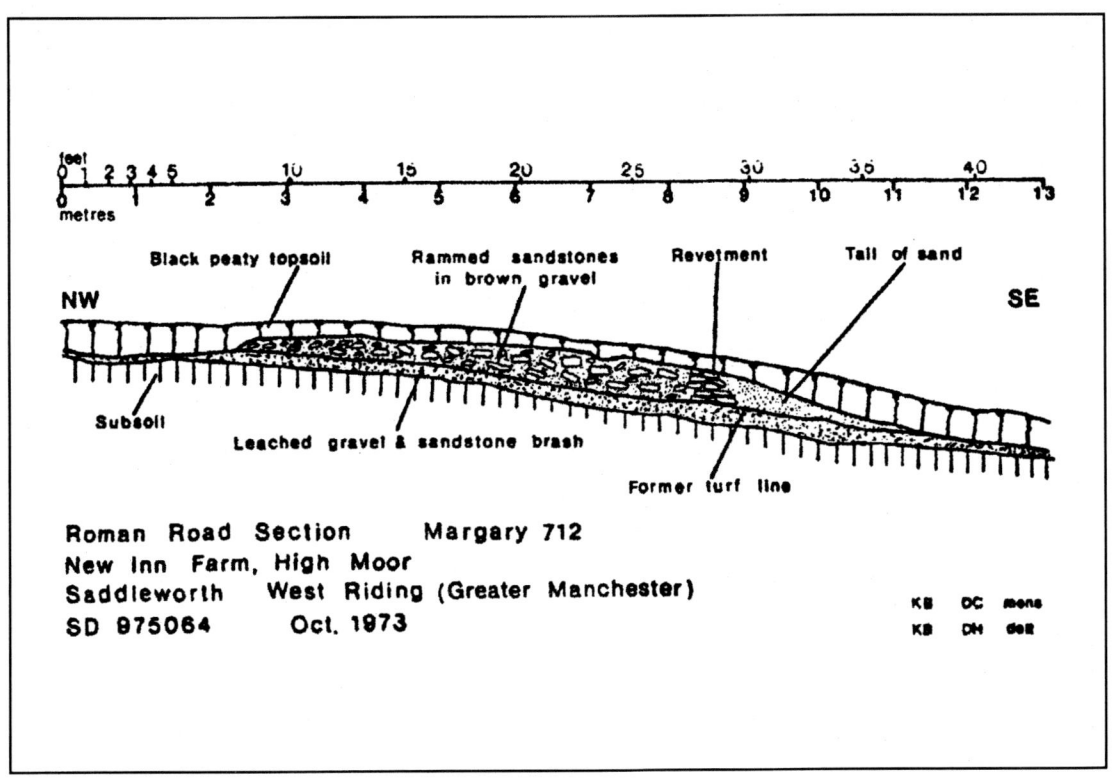

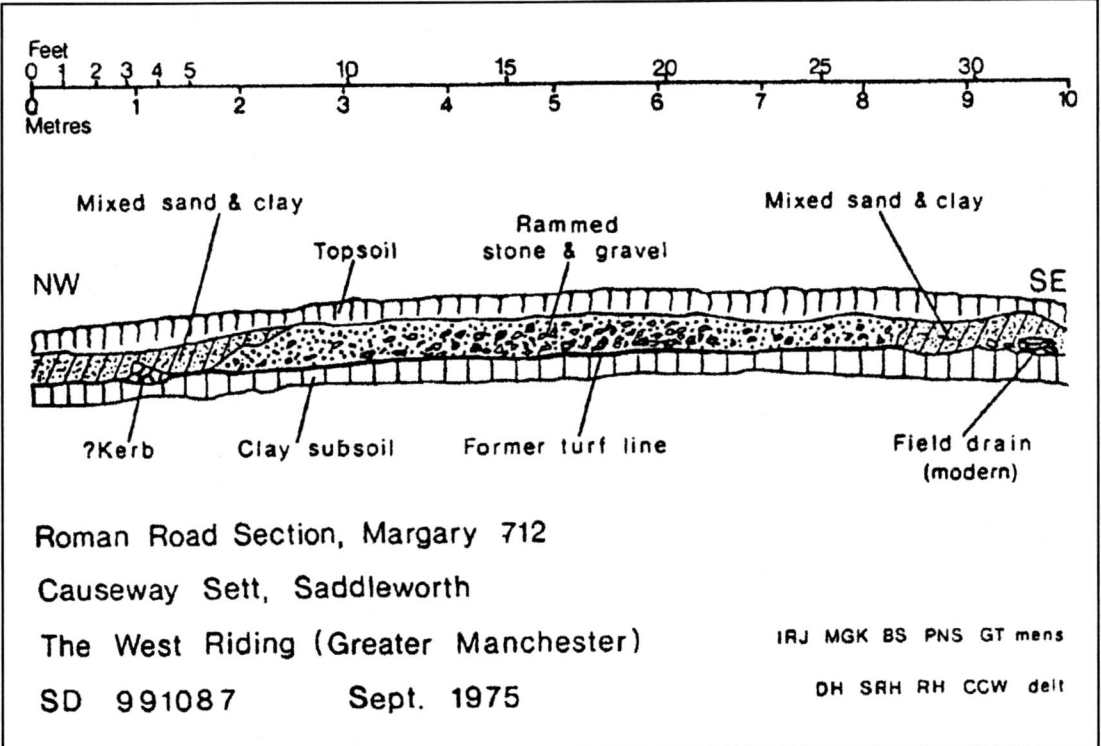

Figure 11 - Roman road excavation sections

From *Saddleworth Seven One Two*

Plate 2 - The agger of the Roman road at Old Nathan's Farm, Austerlands

Plate 3 - The terraceway of the Roman road at Mason Row, Doctor Head.

Plate 4 - The agger of the Roman road at New Inn Farm, High Moor.

The Roman line runs up Cobblers Hill under Delph Lane for a short distance, where the boundary between Friarmere and Lordsmere follows it for about 100yards (91m) before the Roman road leaves Delph Lane on its right and runs directly through the modern houses, via Hull Mill dam to the Castleshaw forts.

If the observer stands in Hull Mill Lane east of the mill dam and looks towards the Castleshaw forts he will see clearly running through the nearer fields traces of the magnificent agger up to 3feet (1m) high and between 40feet (12m) and 50feet (15m) wide, aligned on the south-west corner of the first, larger fort.

Plate 5 - The agger of the Roman road at Hull Mill, Delph

Between Hull Mill and the forts the agger is visible intermittently in the fields and shows clearly on air photographs. In 1975 near Causeway Sett, another significant name, it was excavated revealing rammed stone and gravel set on natural clay. The road foundation material was about 23feet (7m) wide and up to 1.5feet (0.5m) thick and it was set centrally on an agger about 50feet (15m) wide, probably because it was running along a valley bottom prone to swamp and abundant water. There is no doubt that the Roman road across the fields to Castleshaw soon went out of use after Roman repair work ceased, on account of drainage problems, and by the time of the medieval monastic grange in Friarmere, the so-called literary line (which was, in reality, a medieval deviation from the course of the Roman road) had superseded it. The route across the valley bottom is consistent with Percival's account of 1751 but again, not as that interpreted by later writers, including Margary and the Ordnance Survey.

The final approach to the fort runs south of Castle Hill Cote where there is a rather vague piece of agger. Alongside the south wall of the larger fort runs Dry Croft Lane, and south

Plate 6 - The ditches of the Roman road approaching Millstone Edge

Plate 7 - Adeline Clark excavating the Roman road in Oldgate Clough

of this in the field, running not quite parallel to it along its eastern half, is a piece of agger which indicates the start of the next alignment and helps to define the alignment angle as the south west corner of the fort. Link roads certainly led into the first fort by way of the south-west and north-east gates. A geophysical survey carried out in 1977 gave some indication of where the south-western link might be.

Work carried out on the route of the road between the Roman forts at Castleshaw and Slack, found that it passed beneath Castleshaw House on its climb to the summit of Standedge. As the road gained height, the agger was found to be 30feet (7m) to 36feet (11m) wide and varied in height from 1.6feet (0.5m) to 6.5feet (2m). In the field in front of the ruins of Brown Rough Farm, the road turned eastwards and followed the wall to the summit of Millstone Edge. It now turned north again and probably followed the Saddleworth boundary to Oldgate Clough. Here in 1974, excavation revealed a heavy gritstone agger 33feet (10m) wide and up to 1.5feet (0.46m) thick, carrying a road of a width greater than 19.5feet (6m).

After descending Oldgate Clough the Roman road crossed March Haigh Flat beneath Hard Head and, after crossing Burne Moss, began its climb to Cupwith Hill. From Cupwith the alignment crossed Slaithwaite Moor, where two sites, 164feet (50m) apart, were excavated in 1975. The first, a level clay agger 10feet (3m) wide with virtually no metalling, was associated with two deep ditches. At the second site, a slightly cambered clay and gravel agger 19.5feet (6m) wide, again with virtually no metalling, had two shallow ditches.

At New Hey Carrs, the alignment changed and the Roman road passed over Worts Hill. It could be seen from Pole Moor Chapel, descending the hill and passing the graveyard as a narrow raised path. The alignment now turned north-east and, after crossing the present M62 motorway, headed towards Slack Roman fort at Outlane.

In 1974 garden landscaping and subsequent excavation at Winter Hill, close to the Roman fort, revealed the Roman road.

The route of the Roman road from its entry into Saddleworth to the Roman fort at Outlane has therefore been established to follow closely that described by both Percival and Watson in the eighteenth century.

The Environmental Evidence

Since the pioneering work of the 712 Group carried out in the 1970s, the University of Manchester have recently subjected both the Roman road and the vicus at Castleshaw to palaeoenvironmental surveys. The research carried out at the site of the excavation of the Roman road at High Moor has revealed that prior to the building of the road, the land had been cleared by burning. Pollen analysis suggested that the area was partially wooded with areas of open heath and grassland communities. The High Moor analysis came from an upland site and the general absence of cereal pollen would suggest a lack of local arable cultivation prior to the construction of the Roman road. Some cultivation may have been taking place on the lower slopes of the valleys or valley floors but the cereal pollen had not travelled to the High Moor area.

Other Roman roads in Saddleworth

Two other Roman roads are thought to have entered Saddleworth from the south. Both have attracted much literary evidence over the years but to date little archaeological work has been carried out to substantiate their claim to be Roman. Much of what has been written is still subject to discussion and speculation and there is little really joined up evidence according to modern standards of Roman road investigation. The descriptions of the following routes have been summarised from the available literary evidence.

Route 1 Melandra - Buckton - Castleshaw

A road probably left the north gate of the Roman fort at Melandra Castle near Glossop and, after passing the site of the Bath House, crossed the River Etherow and climbed the hillside towards Mottram. On reaching Roe Cross, on the road to Stalybridge, the road headed north and followed the lane through Gallowsclough, Lukes Fold, Flaxfield, Cock Wood and crossed the Brushes valley. The second reservoir up the valley lies over the point where the Roman road crossed. The route of the road is now taken up by a lane which passed through Sun Green and descended the western side of Slatepit Moor to Carrbrook. The line is lost in the valley but is picked up again beneath Buckton Castle. The road now followed the later trackway around the moor, entering Saddleworth at Shadworth Lane (988036) and descended Friezland Lane, crossing the river at Ladhill.

Proceeding by way of Kinders, Knowl, Pobgreen, Runninghill, Diggle, Carr, Hunters Hill and over Harrop Edge, the road crossed the modern A62, descended the fields, and met the Chester to York Roman road (M712) close to Castleshaw Roman fort.

Route 2 Werneth Low - Staley Street - Doctor Lane Head

A road starting an alignment from the Roman camp at Astbury near Congleton, passed across Werneth Low on route to Roe Cross, where it turned towards Stalybridge. Descending from Roe Cross the road followed the line of the current Mottram Old Road, which, on the 1883 Ordnance Survey map was marked Staley Lane. After crossing the River Tame, by way of a ford on the site of the current bridge, the road followed the line of Cocker Hill. After a short distance along the present Wakefield Road, the Roman road turned left towards the modern Glent Quarry and the summit of Ridge Hill Lane.

From here the route followed the ridge towards Mossley, shown on the 1883 Ordnance Survey map as Staley Street, passing on route Arlies Cottages, (where in 1926 a section of an old road was dug up) and Windy Harbour Farm.

After passing through Upper Mossley, the Roman road continued along Quick Edge to Lydgate and Platting Road and, after crossing the present A62 Huddersfield Road, proceeded to Doctor Lane Head where it joined the Roman road from Manchester to Castleshaw, M712.

Plate 8 - The Melandra to Castleshaw Roman road near Buckton Castle

CHAPTER FIVE
The Roman Forts

In this chapter the Castleshaw forts are distinguished as follows:-

1) Earlier larger fort - Castleshaw 1

2) Later smaller fortlet - Castleshaw 2

Discovery and Exploration

In a paper presented to the Royal Society in 1751, Thomas Percival of Royton, after describing the route of the Roman road from Manchester, says: *at Castleshaw I was well pleased to find a double Roman camp.* The paper contained the earliest known plan of the site.

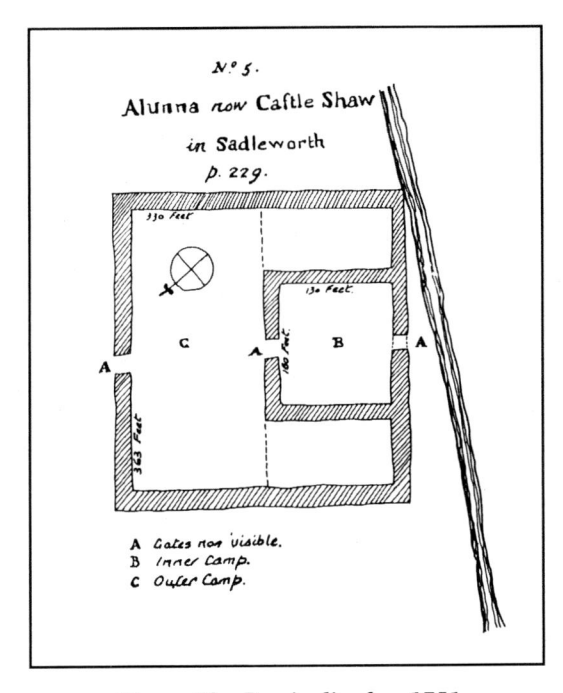

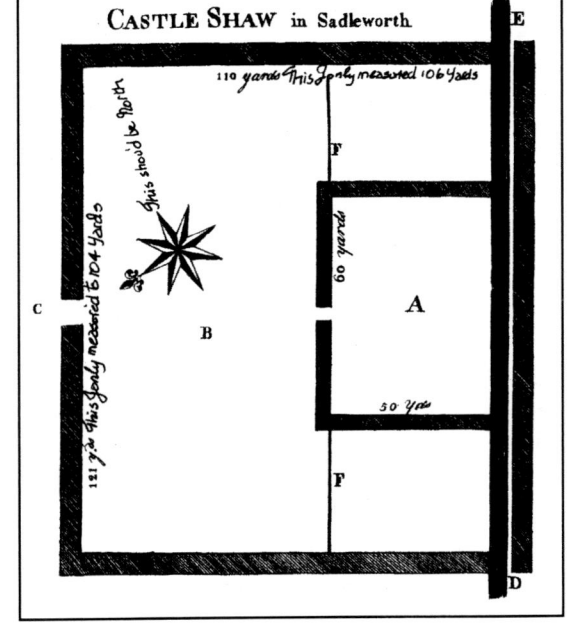

Figure 12 - Percival's plan 1751

Figure 13 - Watson's plan c1766
An adaptation of the plan in Percival's notebook.

The orientation shown on the plans in Figures 12 and 13 is in error by 90 degrees to the west.

In 1766, the Reverend John Watson presented a paper to the Society of Antiquaries. The paper included a simple plan of the Roman forts showing the two sets of ramparts but only one gate, the North Gate of the fort. Perhaps the first excavations at Castleshaw are referred to when the paper reports: *finds of coins, beads, pieces of uncommon pots and bricks had some time ago been found there.*

The Reverend John Whitaker, mentions the site in his History of Manchester published in 1771: *The little station at Castleshaw is very evident on the present track on the way to Slack. -------- The camp at Castleshaw is seated directly at the foot of Stanedge, and within a couple of furlongs from the course of the Roman road. This I have shewn before to have been probably a fortress of the Sistuntii, but to have extended along the area which rises over the rest of the ground, and is all equally denominated the Hus-steads and all defined by the Castlehills. But the Roman station on the site seems to have been contracted into a narrower compass, and to have been inclosed within the foss, that still appears encircling a rounded eminence near the centre, and encompassing about three-fourths of a statute-acre.*

Ammon Wrigley, a local poet and historian tells in his book 'Songs of a Moorland Parish' how he rediscovered the site in 1897. He records having dug *trial holes in various parts of the camp area and was rewarded by finding fragments of Roman tile and pottery.* The camp area referred to is the fortlet (Castleshaw 2) and some of the fragments of Roman tile he found bore incomplete tile stamps, (see chapter 9).

In the summer of 1898, G.F. Buckley a local mill owner of Linfitts, Delph, leased the site for one year and, with the aid of five labourers, began excavating in the fortlet area (Castleshaw 2). He dug a series of diagonal trenches, which produced samian ware, black ware and white ware pottery. A short report of the excavation was placed in the Transactions of the Lancashire and Cheshire Antiquarian Society, Volume 16-1898. The same Society visited the site on the 23th July 1898.

Plate 9 - Ammon Wrigley

The visit marked the close of Buckley's excavations but he gave Wrigley permission to return to the site and continue exploration until the end of the lease in 1899. In actual fact Wrigley continued occasional excavations until 1907 and during this time made further finds of pottery, tiles and two coins.

On July 19th 1907 the site was bought by Samuel Andrew of Lees, a member of the Lancashire and Cheshire Antiquarian Society and Major William Lees of Heywood, a member of the Yorkshire Archaeological Society. Directed by F.A. Bruton, a Classics Master at Manchester Grammar School, they concentrated their efforts on the defences of the fort, (Castleshaw 1) and fortlet, (Castleshaw 2) and the interior layout of the fortlet. Their first interim report of the excavations was published in 1908 followed by a second in 1911. Both reports contained a plan of the site and many splendid photographs. For

Plate 10 - Buckley's excavation 1898

Plate 11 - Samuel Andrew

the first time an accurate layout of some of the buildings and roads within the site was available. Finds from the excavations included samian ware, most types of coarse pottery, a number of Roman coins, remains of leather shoes, a lead lamp holder, timber stakes and a fragment of tile with an incomplete tile stamp. Andrew and Lees had clearly intended to return and continue their explorations. They did return briefly to back-fill some of the trenches left open over the winter, which had been to the detriment of the remains. The majority of the considerable spoil heaps that had resulted from their two seasons of exploration, had remained, making the site totally incomprehensible to the casual visitor.

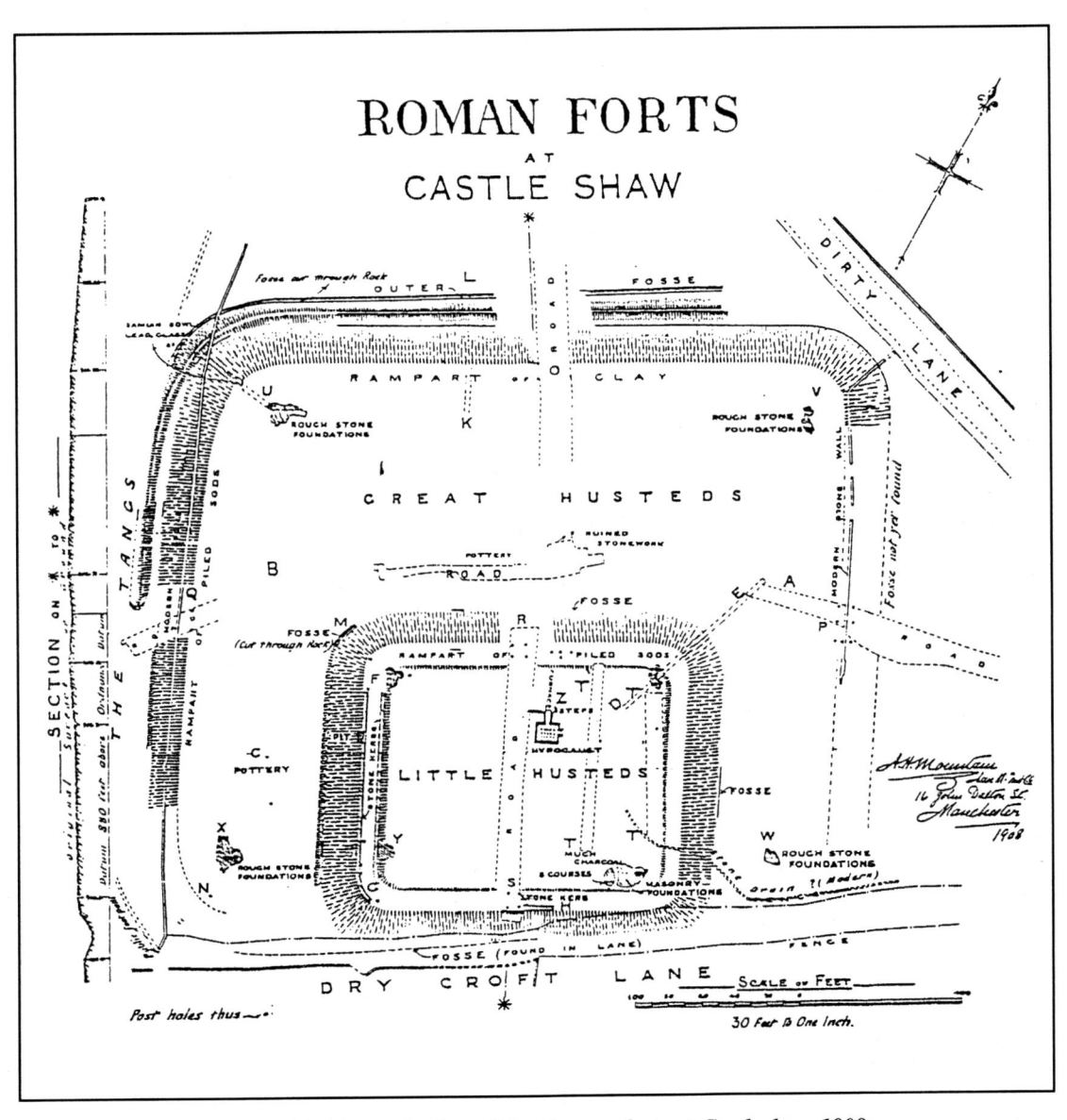

Figure 14 - Bruton's plan of the Roman forts at Castleshaw 1908

Plate 12 - Base of Oven found at the eastern corner of the fortlet

Plate 13 - The Hypocaust Building

Photographs from the Bruton excavations of 1908-09

Plate 14 - Bruton's excavation team at the hypocaust building

Plate 15 - The southern corner of the fortlet showing stone foundation of the rampart

Photographs from the Bruton excavations of 1908-09

Plate 16 - The internal road at the east gate of the fort

Plate 17 - The water channel in the fortlet

Plate 18 - The north rampart of the fort

Photographs from the Bruton excavations of 1908-09

In 1923, Ian Richmond, who later became the doyen of Roman Britain studies, published a paper entitled *The Sequence and Purpose of the Roman Forts at Castleshaw*. He established the dates of the fort (Castleshaw 1) and the fortlet (Castleshaw 2), based mainly on the dateable pottery found on the sites. This dating and the archaeological evidence from the forts enabled the sequence of building to be established. Richmond visited the site in connection with his publication *Huddersfield in Roman Times, 1925*.

The forts then lay neglected until 1957 when archaeology students from Manchester University began a series of training excavations lasting until 1964.

Plate 19 - Ian Richmond

Excavations concentrated in the fort area, (Castleshaw 1) and an interim report in 1957 told of work on the defences. A second interim report in 1961 described buildings found in the north- west corner of the fort. Work finished in 1964 and a final report by F. H. Thompson in the Transactions of the Lancashire and Cheshire Antiquarian Society, Volume 77 - 1967 contained a new plan of the fort, which included details of the interior road system and the positions of the granaries and barracks.

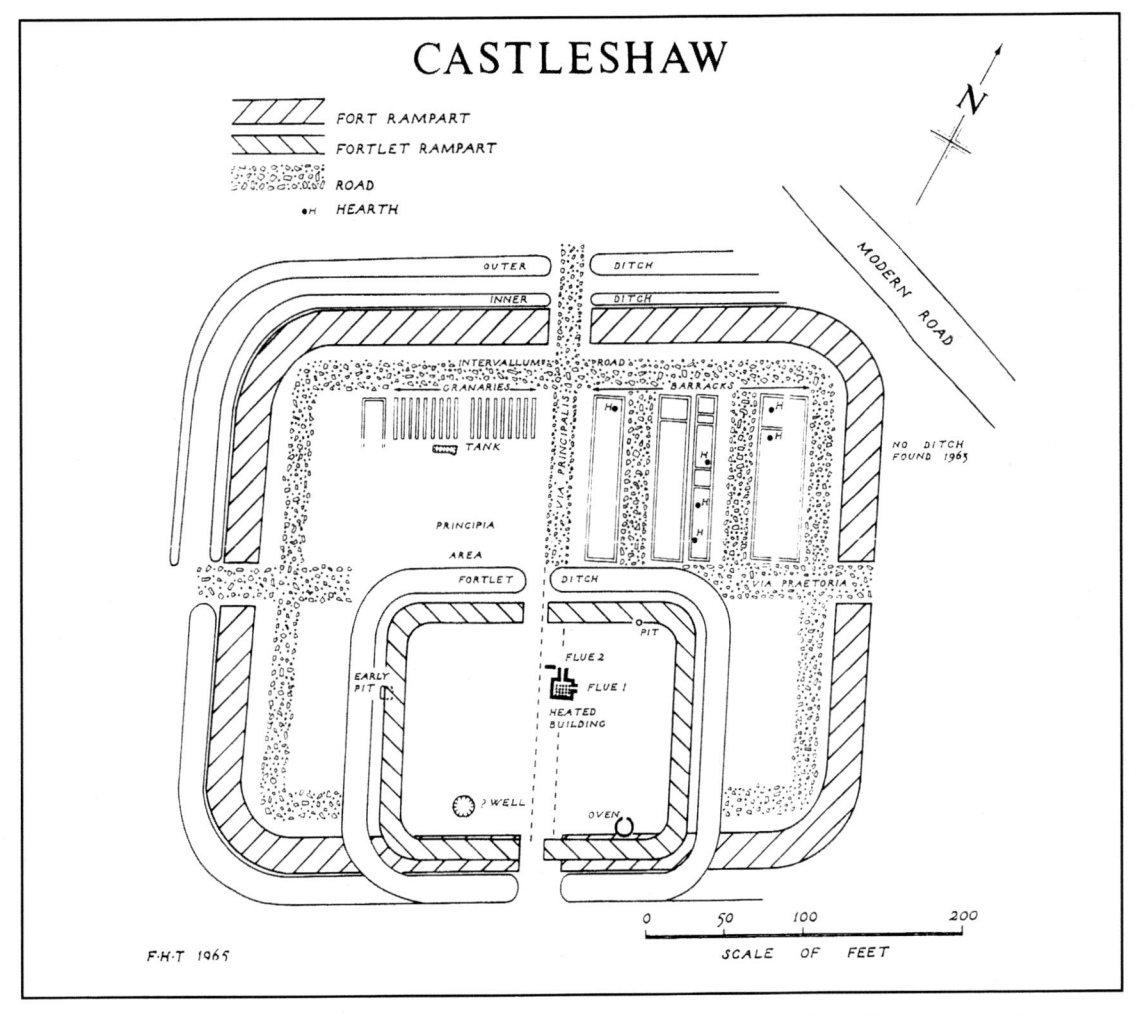

Figure 15 - Conjectural plan of northern half of the fort based on the 1957-64 excavations Drawn by F.H. Thompson

Plate 20 - The main road through the fort (via principalis)

Plate 21 - Details of timber corduroy beneath rampart

Plate 22 - Soak-away formed from an amphora neck

Photographs from the Manchester University excavations of 1957-64

From the information obtained it has been possible to reconstruct the layout of the fort. After the departure of the Manchester University excavation team in 1964, the site was once again left to the ravages of weather and the illegal activities of treasure hunters.

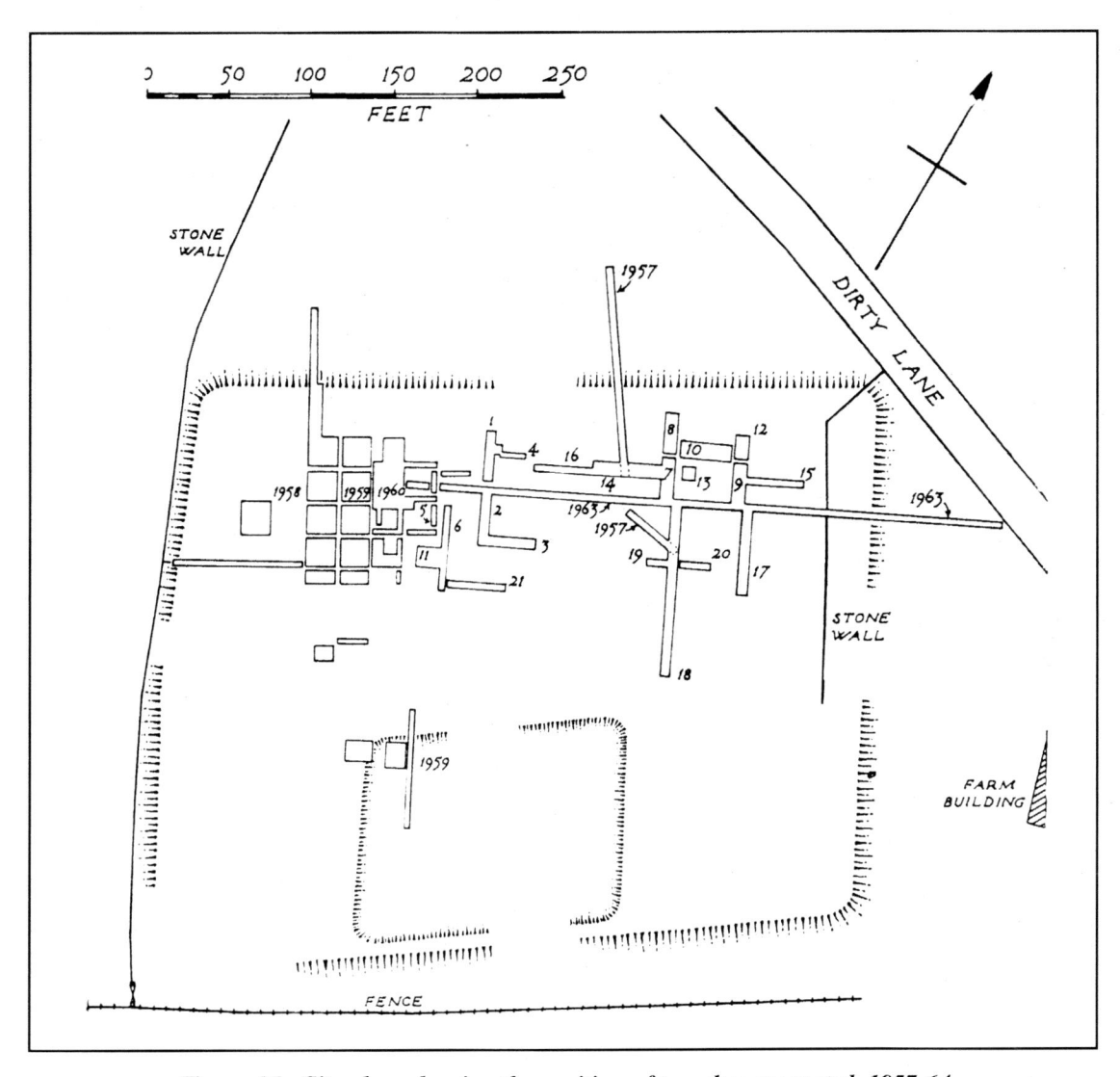

Figure 16 - Site plan, showing the position of trenches excavated, 1957-64

The site was still very difficult to interpret and in 1984 the Greater Manchester Archaeological Unit, with support from the Manpower Services Commission, North West Water, Oldham Metropolitan Borough Council and English Heritage, returned to the site to carry out limited excavations within the fortlet, (Castleshaw 2). Their aims were to subject the site to total restoration and make it both accessible and comprehensible to the general public. Whilst the scope of the exploration allowed was limited to the re-investigation of previous work, excavation in the gateways and several new sections across the ditch system was allowed. This enabled a survey of the ground disturbance before 1985 to take place, and on the plan produced, it was possible to identify the trenches dug by Wrigley, Buckley, Bruton and Thompson. A re-interpretation of the site was possible, and this produced a new and unusual layout.

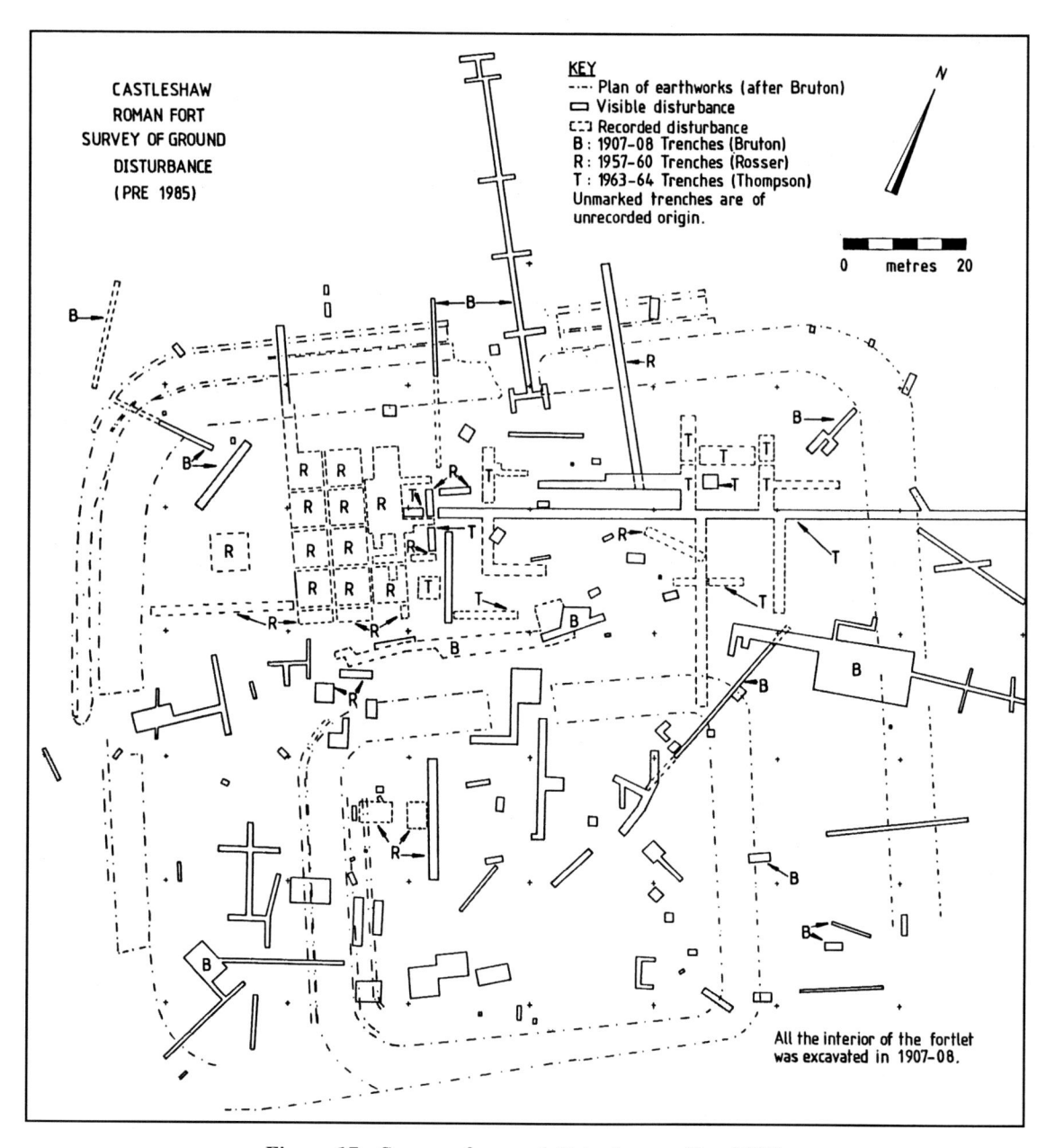

Figure 17 - Survey of ground disturbance. (Pre 1985)

Description of the forts

The Roman forts at Castleshaw saw four main phases of construction during their short occupancy from cAD79 to cAD120.

The fort (Castleshaw 1) revealed, when excavated, evidence of two phases of construction. The Headquarters Building (principia), a room at the end of the store block and the barracks (centuriae) revealed that they had been reconstructed during the life of the fort. During the 1984-88 excavations it was discovered that the western rampart of the fortlet (Castleshaw 2) covered the remains of an oven belonging to the earlier fort (Castleshaw 1). It was also in this area that numerous foundation slots belonging to more than one period of construction were discovered.

Excavation within the fortlet (Castleshaw 2) also revealed two building periods. They coincided with minor alterations rather than reconstruction, and evidence recovered indicated that both the first and second phases of the fortlet shared the same layout.

The Flavian fort (Castleshaw 1)

By the time the final alignment of the Roman road from High Moor was made in AD79, the position of the Roman fort (Castleshaw 1) was known. If the fort had not previously been constructed, it had certainly been marked out on the ground, which enabled the alignment of the road to be made to the south-west corner.

Castleshaw 1 was a typical turf and timber auxiliary fort with the four corners facing the cardinal points. An auxiliary fort was normally designed to hold an auxiliary unit of the Roman army. These were non-legionary regiments recruited from the provincial peoples of the Roman Empire. Unit strength would be either 500 or 1000 men. The measurements inside the ramparts were approximately 361 feet (110m) x 298 feet (91m), enclosing an area of almost 2.47 acres (1 hectare).

It has been argued that the fort was founded in AD79 and was abandoned after a brief occupation, lying empty during the last decade of the first century. No inscription or tile stamp has been found that would give any clue to the identity of the occupants of the fort during this period.

The fort layout followed the standard pattern and would be capable of housing a cohort (500 men). Infantry would predominate but the garrison was probably supplied with a small mounted detachment, perhaps consisting of one centuria (80men), as at the sister fort at Slack, near Huddersfield. The fort lay alongside the Roman road and had branch roads entering both west and east gates. Of the fort's internal roads or streets, the main one, *the via principalis*, ran north to south, the road from the south gate joining the main Chester to York road (M712). A road has been traced leaving the north gate for a short distance, but any further evidence was destroyed when the reservoirs were constructed in 1887.

The Fort Defences

The Ditches (Fossae) - Two ditches were present on the north and west sides of the fort, the inner and outer ditches were both V-shaped in section. Their width was 6 feet (1.8m) and 11 feet (3.3m) respectively, and their depth 2.5 feet (0.76m) and 3 feet (0.91m). A berm, or flat space of ground, of 7 feet (2.1m) separated the inner ditch from the rampart. On the south-west and southern side a single ditch only was found, some what confused with the later Dry Croft Lane, which over-lies the ditch. To-date no ditch has been found on the east side of the fort.

The Ramparts (Vallum) - The rampart, about 17 feet (5.2m) in width at its base, was built of turf laid on a raft of transverse horizontal oak posts (commonly known as a corduroy), for stability. It is possible that the rampart would have been 12.5 feet (3.8m) high to the walkway or fighting platform, which would have been protected by a crenellated breastwork 6.5 feet (2m) in height. Timber staircases *(ascensi)* would have provided access to the rampart walk.

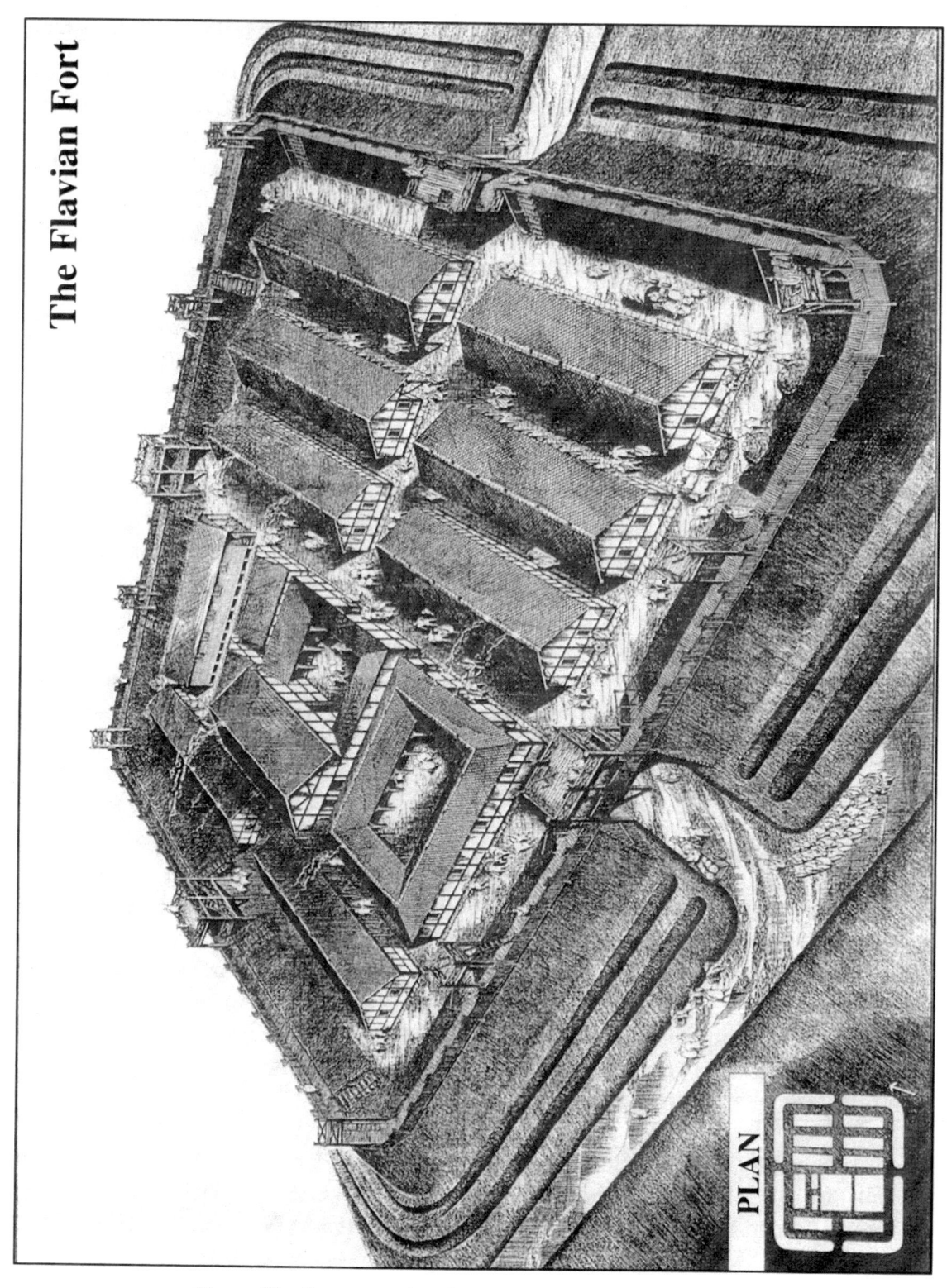

Figure 18 - Reconstruction drawing of the fort (Castleshaw 1)

The Corner Towers - Corner towers or turrets are a common feature of Roman forts. Evidence, found in 1907, of blocks of masonry in each corner of the fort, may suggest the foundations for timber turrets. The turrets would rise above the rampart-walk to provide lookout or signalling towers.

The Gateways (Portae) - There were four gateways, one in the centre of each rampart. They were all built of timber and, apart from the south gate, which appeared to have a single chamber, they were without guard chambers. The rampart walkway would bridge across the gateways and it is likely that there would be a tower at a higher level above each gate. The north gate was found to have a single portal, the other three gates had double portals.

The Fort Interior

The Internal Roads - Most of our knowledge about the internal layout of auxiliary forts derives from a third century AD manual written by the classical author and surveyor, Hyginus *(hyginus gromaticus)*. The fort at Castleshaw conformed in layout to that specified in this manual and the arrangement of the internal roads, streets and buildings are as shown on the plan, (fig 19). Of the roads shown on Bruton's plan of 1908 (fig 14) only the one leaving the north gate pertained to the fort period. The other roads were all contemporary of the fortlet phase when, at some later stage the Chester to York road was diverted through the abandoned fort. This diversion was made to avoid the civil settlement *(vicus)* outside the south gate.

The Headquarters Building (Principia) - This was the administrative and religious centre of the fort. It was positioned centrally opposite the junction of the two principal streets and facing the front gate. The standard plan was an open courtyard at the front surrounded by a veranda, a cross-hall, and five rooms to the rear. First century timber headquarters buildings tended to be simpler, sometimes omitting the cross-hall and possessing only three rooms at the rear. The central room, the *aedes* served as a shrine and normally contained a statue of the emperor, the standards of the unit and the pay chest. Administrative staff used the rooms on either side. The fort (Castleshaw 1) has been described as a 'rough and ready establishment' and it is likely that this building would have been of very simple design and construction, - timber walls, simple thatch or shingled roof and a pounded earth floor. The overall size could have been in the region of 65.5 feet (20m) square. This building lies partially beneath the ditches and north-west rampart of the later fortlet (Castleshaw 2) and evidence of its existence was revealed during the 1984-88 excavations.

The Commander's House (Praetorium) - This is sited adjacent to the headquarters building, now covered by the western half of the fortlet (Castleshaw 2). The standard design is a central courtyard surrounded by the rooms that formed the living accommodation of the unit commander and his family. One room was normally reserved for receiving official visitors. Again, this building would have been of simple design and construction, timber and either thatch or shingle roof with an earth floor. The size would be in the region of 65.5 feet (20m) square. This building was partly revealed during the 1984-88 excavations in the fortlet area beneath the granary and courtyard building.

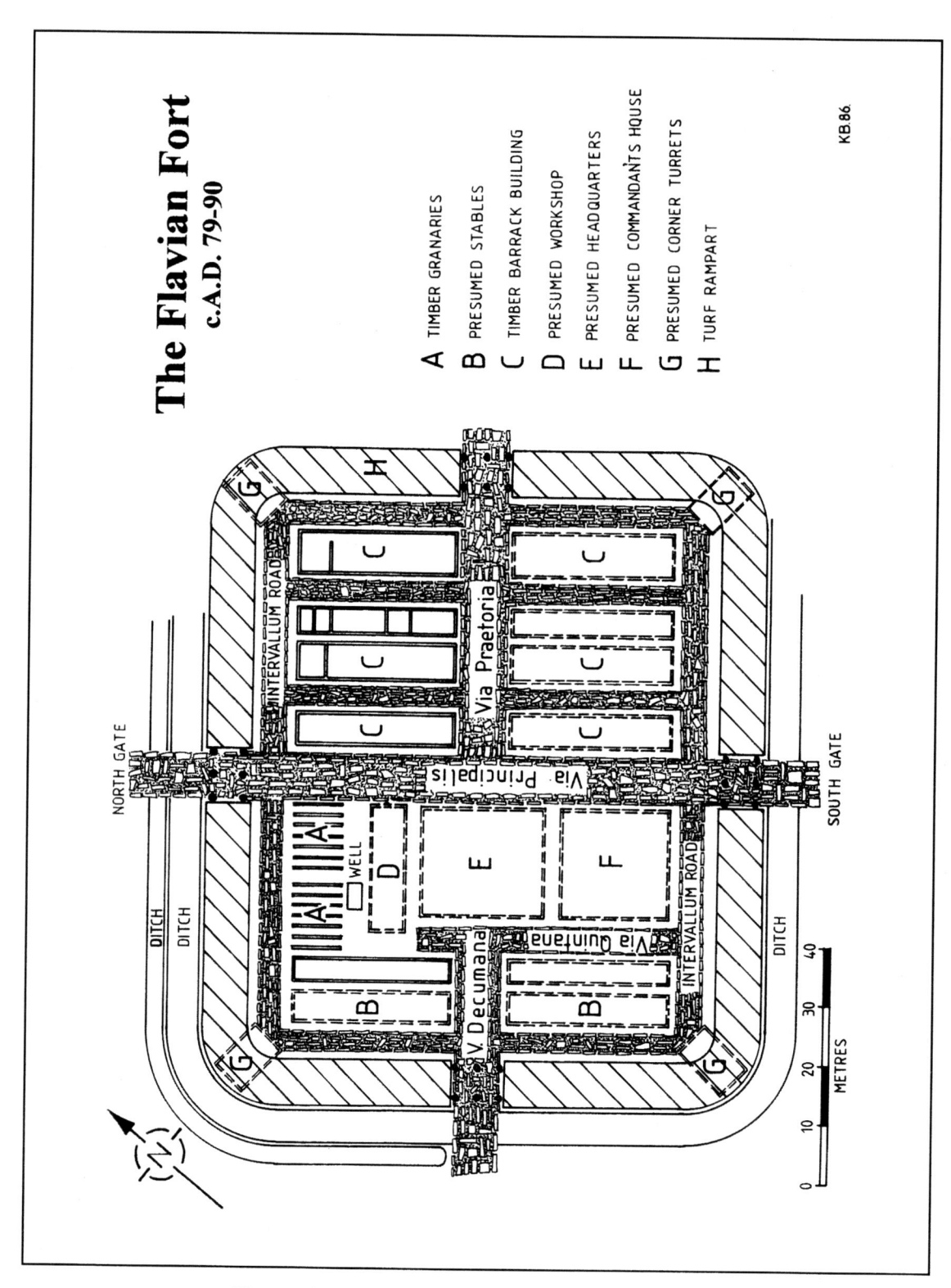

Figure 19 - Conjectural plan of the fort (Castleshaw 1)

The Granaries (Horrea) - Two granaries were found in the north-west quarter of the fort adjacent to the intervallum road (the road between the rampart and the internal buildings) arranged on a west-east axis. They were constructed from timber, the floor raised above ground level on timber posts to prevent both dampness and vermin. The granary walls had louvered panels at high level to assist with ventilation and the roofs probably covered with timber shingles.

Covered loading bays were situated at one end of each granary to make it easier to transfer quantities of grain from carts to the interior of the granary. Each granary was approximately 39 feet (12m) x 29 feet (9m) and would be capable of holding one year's supply of grain for the garrison of the fort.

The Barracks (Centuriae) - The front and rear areas of the fort were reserved for barracks. From evidence obtained in the 1957-64 excavations the buildings were 110 feet (33.5m) long x 20 feet (6.1m) wide (small for a typical auxiliary barrack block). Each barrack had ten rooms to house the eighty men of each century and quarters for the centurion at one end of the barrack. Each of the ten rooms would be divided into a small front area *(arma)* for the storage of arms and equipment and a larger rear area *(papilio)* where the eight men lived and slept. It was normal for this area to contain a hearth for heating and cooking. The barrack buildings were of timber construction with either a thatch or shingle roof covering and the flooring was probably of pounded earth (as at Slack, the next fort along the road) which had the advantage of warmth over some of the more elaborate finishes. A hole covered with a timber shutter in the rear wall provided lighting and ventilation.

The Stables - The presence of cavalry and the need for pack animals at Castleshaw would suggest the presence of stable blocks. Very little is known about stables within Roman forts and nowhere has there been found sufficient evidence to show the complete layout of a fort's stable accommodation. At Castleshaw scant remains of a timber building 10 feet (3m) wide x 98 feet (30m) long were exposed during the 1957-64 excavations in the northwest quarter of the fort. It is likely that this building is one of the pair of stables that would be necessary to house the animals present. A similar layout was found at Slack, again in the northwest quarter. The stables at Castleshaw would have been constructed from timber with thatched roofs and earth floors.

Other buildings would be present at Castleshaw (1) but to date only limited archaeological evidence is available, since only 35% of the fort has been examined.

Below is a list of these buildings with an assumption made as to their position within the fort layout.

Workshop (Fabrica) - This would have been situated between the headquarters building and the granaries (as at Slack) and used by both metalworkers and carpenters for the manufacture of items required in the routine maintenance of the fort defences and internal buildings. Fixtures and furniture for the buildings within the fort would also be manufactured in the workshop. The adjacent water tank was probably associated with the activities of the workshop.

Storehouses - Storage facilities would have been required within the fort to house the wide range of equipment and provisions necessary to ensure the well being of the garrison. The storehouses were probably situated adjacent to the Via Quintana, (the road running at the rear of the principal buildings).

Latrines - The communal latrine was normally placed against the rampart, at the lowest part of the fort. At Castleshaw this would be in the south-west corner and a drain beneath the rampart would allow the sewage to be carried away. The latrine building would be a simple timber and thatch construction but no excavation has taken place in this area of the fort and its location can only be supposition.

Water Supply - Little or no consideration has been given in the past to the water supply to the Roman fort at Castleshaw. The garrison would require a considerable quantity of fresh water, estimated at 0.55 gallons (2.5litres) per man, per day, for washing, drinking and cooking. Additional supplies of water would be required for use by the horses present, the flushing of the latrines and the requirements of the bathhouse. The Castleshaw valley is not short of water and in the recent past the streams descending the hillside from Millstone Edge fed a number of water powered mills in the valley. During the excavations by Bruton in 1907, a covered stone water channel was discovered entering the fort at its south-east angle and was traced for a short distance. The excavators thought that it might have been modern, but in construction it is typical of Roman work and similar to that found at the Roman forts at Birrens and High Rochester. Fresh water might have been collected from one of the many streams or springs in the immediate area and piped into the fort by means of this channel.

Ovens - No report has been made of finding ovens in the fort, but they must have been present. Normally they were set into the rear of the ramparts and a number would have been required to satisfy the needs of a cohort strength garrison (480 men). The ovens would comprise a circular base 10 feet (3m) in diameter built to a flagged hearth height of 1.6 feet (0.5m). It is thought that a dome-shaped structure covered the flag floor and that a fire of wood would be lit on this floor and allowed to burn until the interior of the oven was thoroughly heated. The charcoal would then be removed, the bread inserted and the door to the oven tightly sealed until baking had been completed. There were no communal messes in Roman forts so the troops would either dine in the open or in their barrack-rooms. In the 1984-88 excavations, traces of an oven were found beneath the western rampart of the fortlet. The close proximity of this oven to the commander's house may suggest that it was for the use of the *praetorium*.

The abandonment of the fort

It is thought that the fort (Castleshaw 1) was abandoned in the last decade of the first century, about AD90. About this time the Roman army was withdrawing from Scotland and reorganising the defence of northern Britain. It had lost one of the four original legions, the 2nd Adiutrix, which had been posted to the Dacian wars. It might be that the garrison of the fort at Castleshaw was moved north to help consolidate the new frontier, or assist in the manning of the newly acquired territory in what is now known as the Lake District.

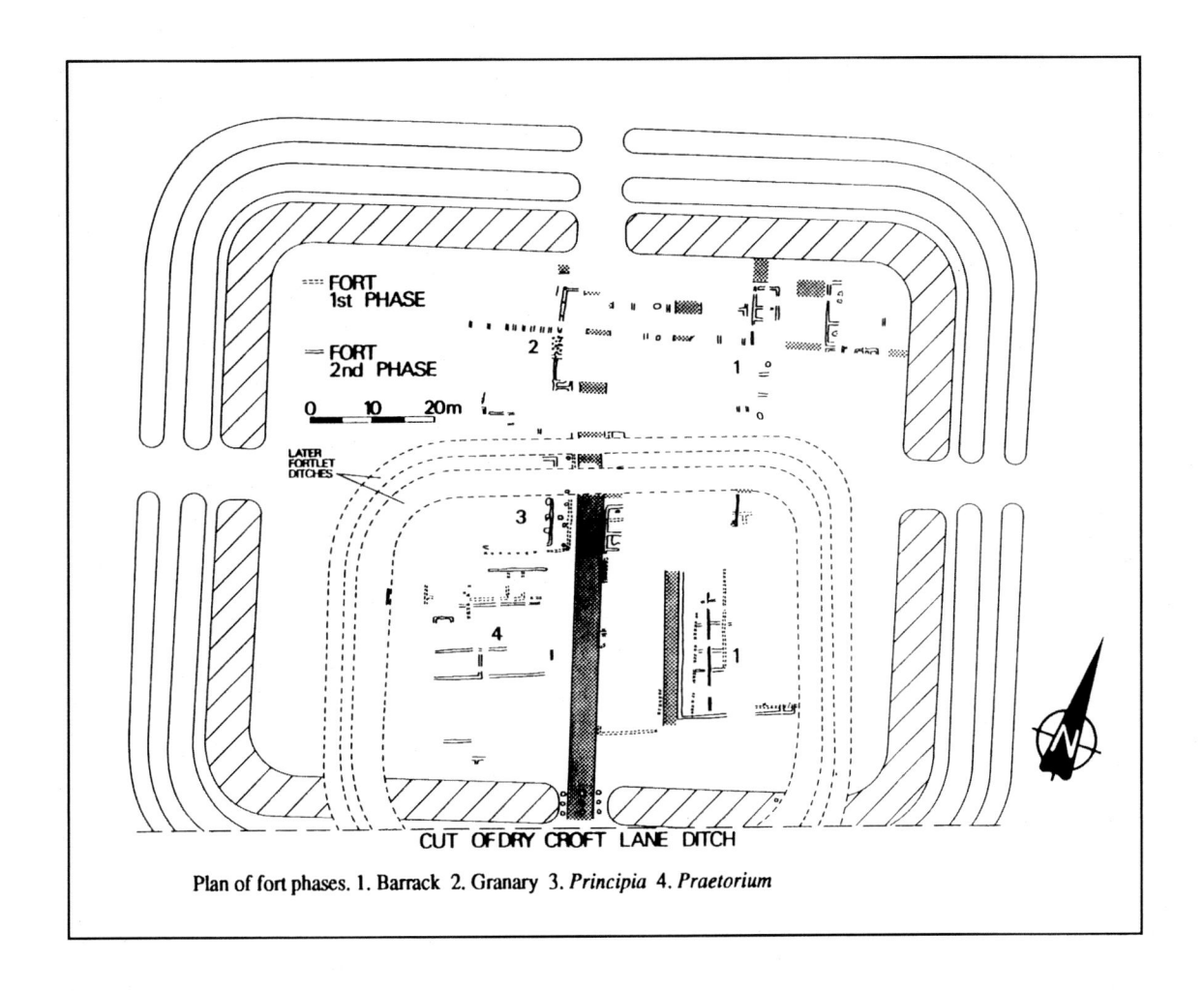

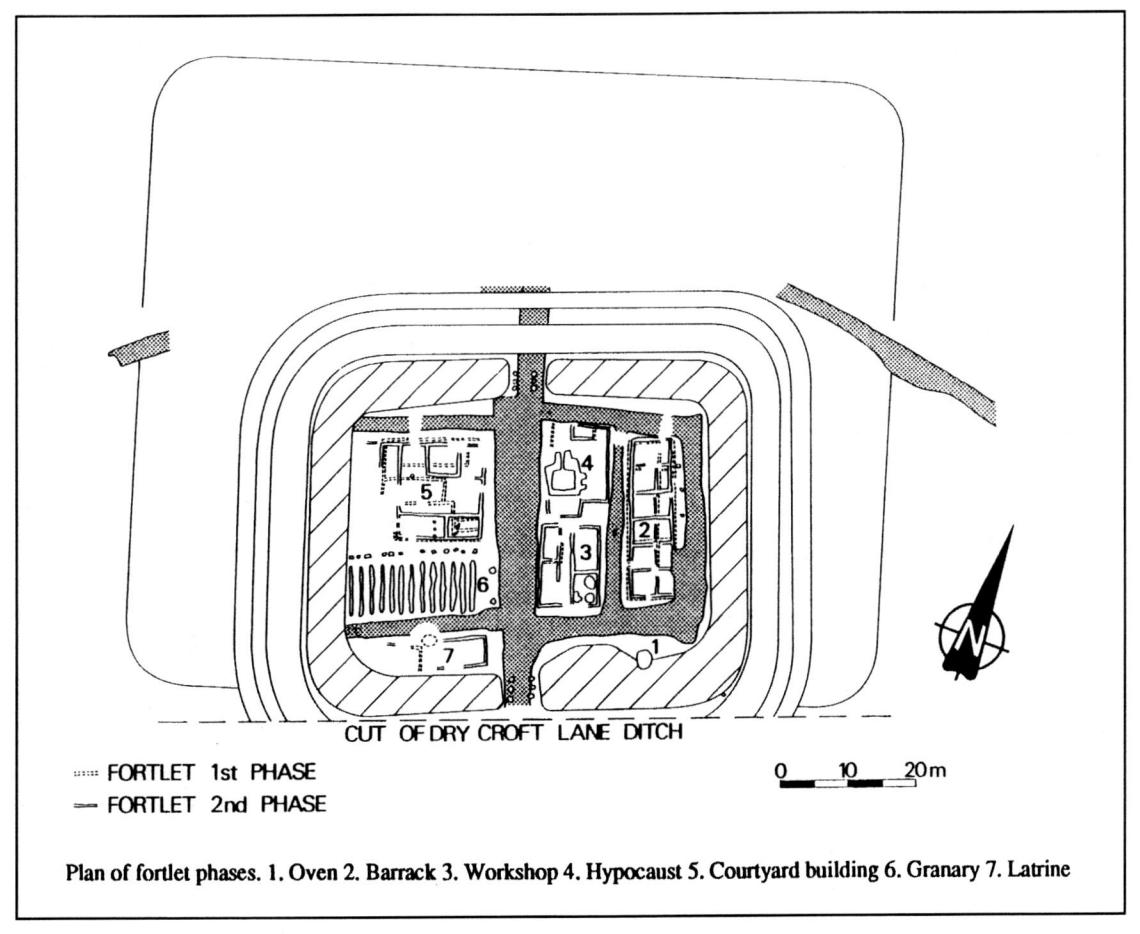

Plan of fort phases. 1. Barrack 2. Granary 3. *Principia* 4. *Praetorium*

Plan of fortlet phases. 1. Oven 2. Barrack 3. Workshop 4. Hypocaust 5. Courtyard building 6. Granary 7. Latrine

Figure 20 - The building phases of the fort and fortlet

The Trajanic fortlet (Castleshaw 2)

Coinciding with the abandonment of the majority of the Scottish lowland forts a new frontier was established in the early years of the second century. This frontier followed the line of the Stanegate road, which ran from Corbridge in the east to Carlisle in the west. The re-organisation caused changes in the deployment of the Roman garrisons in Brigantia. The site at Castleshaw was re-occupied and a small fortlet (Castleshaw 2) was built within the remains of the fort (Castleshaw 1), sharing a section of the southern defences. The fortlet measured approximately 164 feet (50m) x 131 feet (40m) inside the ramparts, enclosing an area of almost 0.5 acres (0.2 hectares). The generally accepted date of the foundation of the fortlet (Castleshaw 2) is cAD 105. The forts situated either side of Castleshaw, Manchester to the west and Slack to the east were both occupied at this time, perhaps giving some indication of the importance of the Roman road connecting the legionary fortresses at Chester and York, which now lay much closer to the northern frontier.

The Fortlet Defences

The Ditches (Fossae) - Two ditches of Punic type surround the fortlet separated by a berm 6.5 feet (2m) in width. The inner ditch was 12.8 feet (3.9m) wide x 4.26 feet (1.3m) deep and the outer ditch was 8.2 feet (2.5m) x 3 feet (0.9m) deep. The Punic ditch form had a steep, almost vertical, outer scarp with a gentler inner slope. This profile may have been intended to lure an attacker within range of missiles from the rampart, with an apparently easy slope to climb. The steeper outer scarp however, being far more difficult to negotiate, hindered his retreat and kept him within missile range for as long as possible. An anomaly noticed during the 1984 excavations was a groove 0.65 feet (0.2m) deep x 0.98 feet (0.3m) wide cut into the inner face of the ditch at the eastern corner of the defences. The slot, half way up the gentle slope of the inner ditch, may have been a defensive feature called a curvus. Thorn branches or sharpened boughs were fixed into the groove, providing additional obstacles for potential attackers. Near the west corner of the fortlet a further anomaly was discovered in a trench being dug across the two ditches. In the base of the inner ditch (the ditch nearest the rampart), two slots now considered 'ankle breakers' were exposed. One of the slots terminated in the trench whilst the other passed through. The explanation for this may be that two construction crews, who were digging the ditch independently, met at this point.

Plate 23 - The Bruton spoil heaps before the restoration of the fortlet.

The Ramparts (Vallum) - The rampart, about 23 feet (7m) in width at its base was built of turf laid on a rubble foundation. It is possible that the rampart would have been 11.8 feet (3.6m) high to the walkway or fighting platform, which would have had a width of 6.5 feet (2m) and be protected by a crenellated breastwork 6.5 feet (2m) high.

The Corner Towers - During the 1908 excavations evidence was found of rough coursed stonework in each of the corners of the fortlet but scant evidence of any post-holes (a hole made in the ground to receive a wooden post and sometimes packed with stones or clay for support). The remains were so slight that nothing definite could be discovered of the plan of the corner towers. Again in 1984 the excavators experienced the same problems and found only one post-hole at the eastern corner. Evidence for corner towers is normally in the form of either four or six post-holes at the rampart corners and whilst they are a common feature in forts, little is known about their occurrence in fortlets. It may well be that they were deemed unnecessary at Castleshaw 2 and that the towers above the gateways sufficed for lookouts and signalling.

The Gateways (Portae) - There were two opposing gateways, centrally placed in the north and south ramparts of the fortlet and connected together with a paved road, which passed through the fortlet *(via principalis)*. The north gate was single portal (one gate), flanked by three pairs of posts and 6.89 feet (2.1m) wide.

Plate 24 - The Punic ditch and curvus at the south-east corner of the fortlet revealed during the 1984-88 excavations.

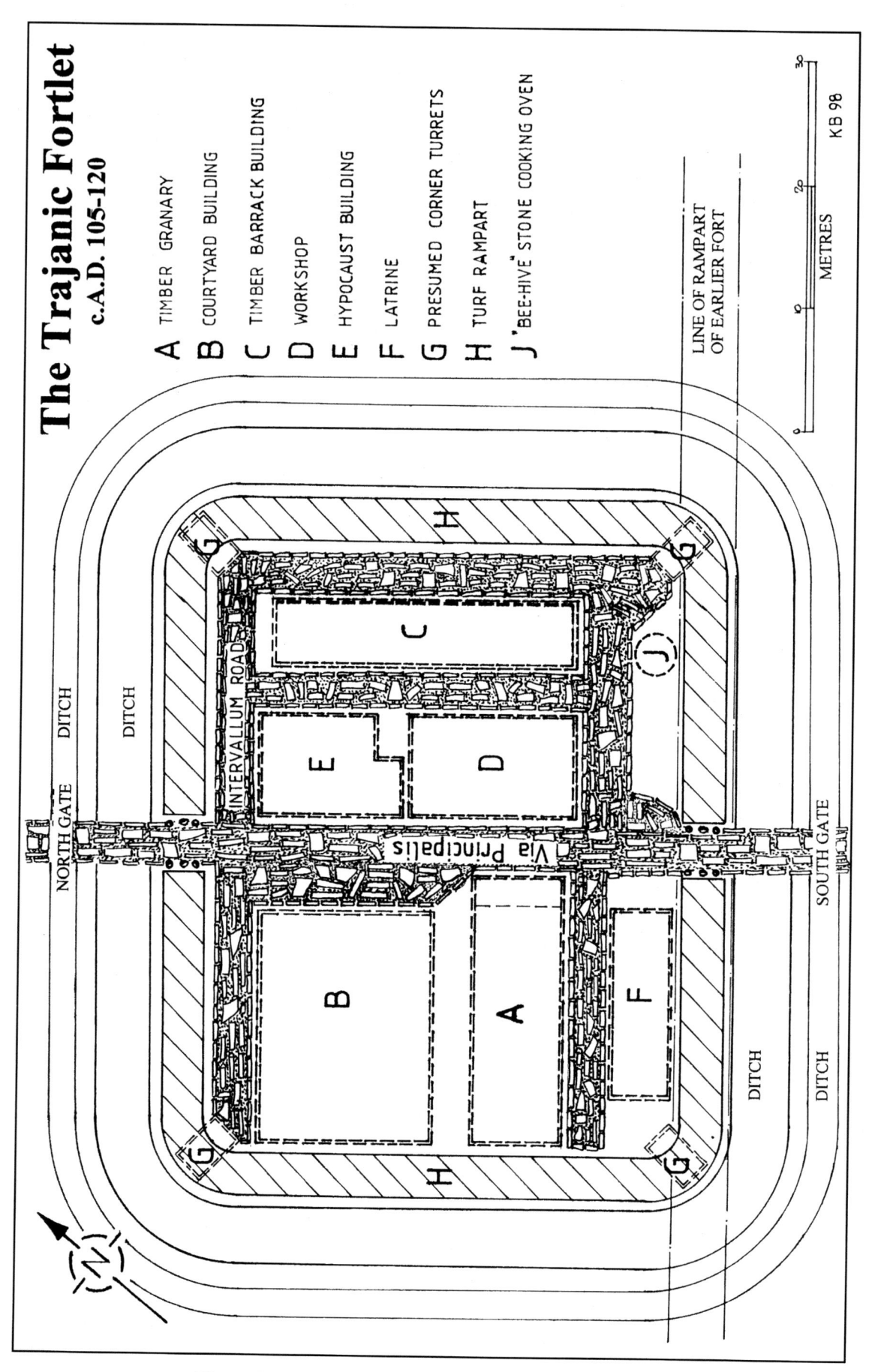

Figure 21 - Conjectural plan of the fortlet (Castleshaw 2)

The central post-holes had survived Bruton's excavations in 1907 and when excavated in 1984-88 they indicated that the upright timbers of the gateway were in the order of 8 inches square (0.2m). They had been set in stone and clay packed post-holes to a depth of 2 feet (0.6m). The south gate was of similar arrangement to the north gate but this time it was 8.86 feet wide (2.7m). Both gates were wide enough to allow wagons to pass through. Each of the ditches surrounding the fortlet passed across the gateways without break. It must be presumed that timber bridges would be used to cross the ditches. The gateways would normally have towers for lookouts and signalling.

Plate 25 - The north gateway of the fortlet. 1984-88.

The Fortlet Interior

The Internal Roads - The 1908 plan of the fortlet indicated three internal roads, (fig14). The most recent excavations of 1984-88 confirmed their existence and also the presence of a continuous intervallum road along the north, east and south-east sides of the fortlet but, unusually, absent on the west and south-west sides. The layout of the roads divided the fortlet interior into three areas, (fig 21). The main road through the fortlet, the *via principalis*, connected the two gateways and was built using the main road of the earlier fort as a foundation. Whilst not as wide as the earlier road, with the exception of the area fronting the courtyard building, a further reduction in width was required before passing through the single portal gateways. A second road lay in the eastern sector of the site, separating the hypocaust and workshop buildings from the barrack block. This again was a re-used fort road, overlying a road discovered by Thompson in his excavations of 1957-64. This section of road varied in width from 8.2 feet (2.5m) to 4 feet (1.2m). There was little need for this road as the buildings on each side could be accessed from either the *via principalis* or the intervallum road. A road in the western sector of the fortlet passed between the granary and the latrine building, terminating at the western rampart.

Plate 26 - The two ditch slots, perhaps the junction of two construction teams. 1984-88

Plate 27 - The post-holes and road surface at the south gate. 1984-88

The latrine building occupied the space between the road and the rear of the south-west rampart.

The fortlet road system would appear to follow the basic principles laid down for military sites with the exception of the absence of an intervallum road behind the west and south-west defences. The insertion of the courtyard building, overlarge granary and latrine building at the expense of the intervallum road, suggest that military activities were perhaps of secondary importance.

Plate 28 - The intervallum road running inside the east rampart

The Barracks (Centuriae) - A single barrack building was found in the eastern half of the fortlet, adjacent to the intervallum road. It measured approximately 75.5 feet (23m) long x 19.7 feet (6m) wide and contained six sets of rooms *(contubernia)*, each measuring approximately 11.5 feet (3.5m) x 17.7 feet (5.4m) internally. The internal arrangements were very similar to those described for the barracks in the fort (Castleshaw 1). From the evidence of this barrack building it can be assumed that the garrison strength of the fortlet (Castleshaw 2) would be in the region of 40-48 men.

The Hypocaust Building - Excavation in 1908 revealed a two-phase stone hypocaust measuring 10 feet (3m) x 11.5 feet (3.5m) internally. It had been re-floored and the position of the flue moved during the occupancy of the fortlet. On three sides of the hypocaust building, excavation revealed the construction trenches of timber buildings. It was first thought to be a small bathhouse type building but, due to the lack of infrastructure to support a bathhouse, it must be considered that the possible occupant of the heated building was the commanding officer of the fortlet. The stone building containing the hypocaust had a tiled roof, the timber buildings would have had either thatch or shingle roofs.

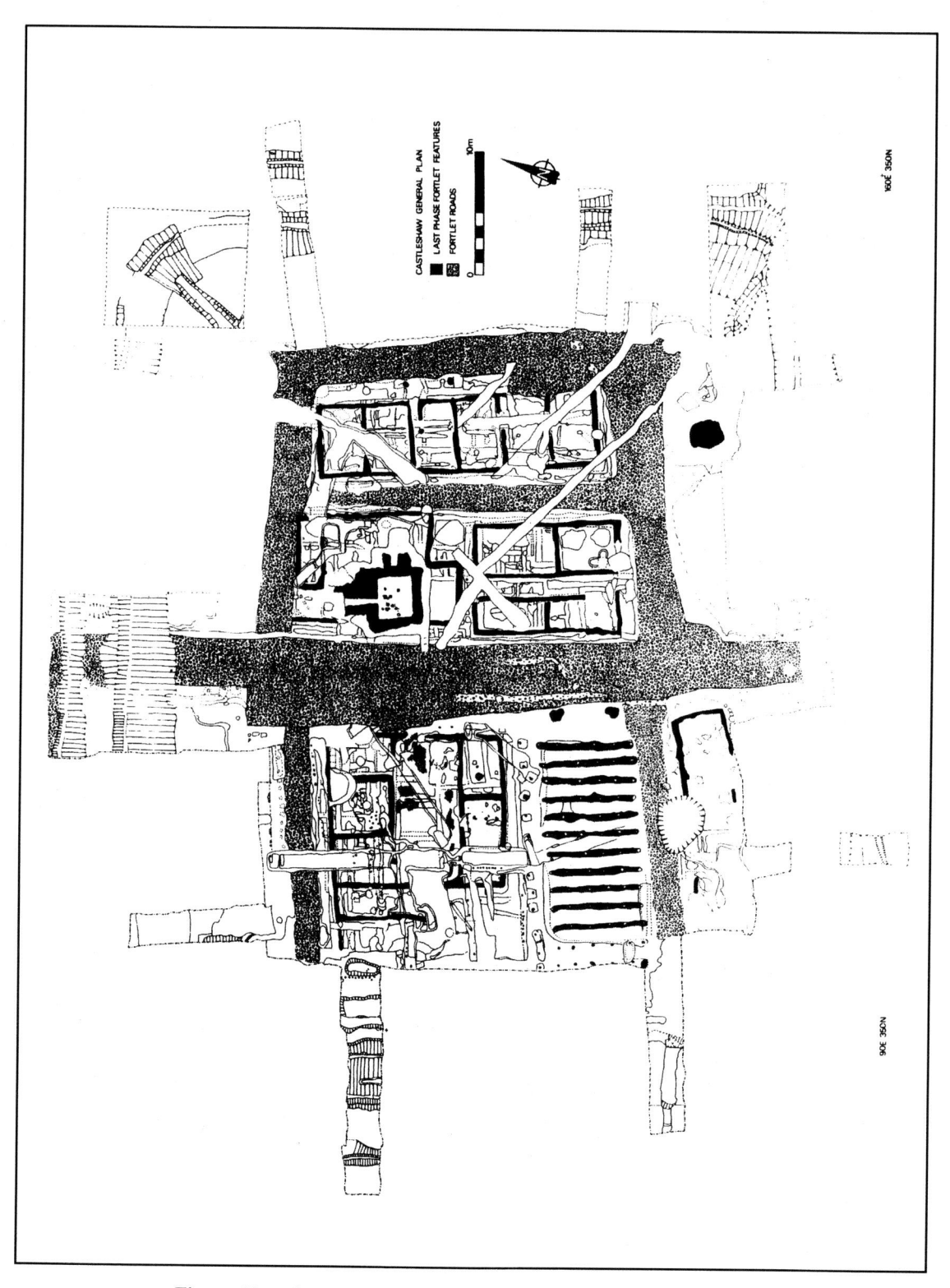

Figure 22 - Plan of the fortlet (Castleshaw 2) excavations. 1984-88

The Workshop (Fabrica) - Situated behind the hypocaust building and alongside the *via principalis* (the main road through the fortlet), excavation revealed construction trenches of a rectangular corridor building, 44.3 feet (13.5m) long x 31 feet (9.5m) wide. Part of this building had been used as a workshop, evidenced by a number of pits which had been used for metalworking activities, probably blacksmithing rather than smelting. Again the building would have been of timber construction with a shingle roof.

The Oven - Originally revealed during the 1908 excavations, a stone built oven was set into the back of the rampart near the south-east corner of the fortlet. It belonged to the type of domed oven found in many forts and fortlets in Britain. The dimensions of the surviving remains were 9 feet (2.75m) in diameter and a height of 2 feet (0.61m) to the stone paved floor. Above this floor would have been a dome of rough stones packed with clay and a small hob would have been built at the front of the oven. The operation of the oven would have been as that of the Flavian fort. (Castleshaw 1)

The Courtyard Building - In the north-west quarter of the fortlet remains of a courtyard building were discovered. Whilst this area was much disturbed, it was possible to recover evidence of at least four building phases. The structure had its entrance on the east side and the north and south wings could be identified with some certainty. The courtyard between the wings, an area of 39 feet (12m) x 16.4 feet (5m), was laid with small rounded cobblestones. The eastern boundary of the building was walled with a paved entranceway connected to the *via principalis*. The west wing connected the north and south wings and was presumably a taller structure. The overall size of the courtyard building was about 46 feet (14m) x 59 feet (18m), the north wing being 39 feet (12m) x 16 feet (5m), the south wing 39 feet (12m) x 13 feet (4m) and the west wing 46 feet (14m) x 19.7 feet (6m). The north wing contained four rooms, some with hearths, and it is thought that the south wing which had two rooms, may have contained stables.

The building was of timber construction with a thatch or shingle roof. Whilst the purpose of this building can only be speculative (courtyard buildings in British fortlets are rare) it could be seen as a multi-purpose structure catering for both official travellers passing between York (Eboracum) and Chester (Deva), together with the administrative requirements of the fortlet.

The Granary Building (Horrea) - The granary, which lay adjacent to the courtyard building, was a major building within the fortlet. The Roman surveyors had dug out a flat rectangular platform before the building was erected. Its capacity was far in excess of the requirements of the garrison. The timber building was 61 feet (18.5m) long x 24.5 feet (7.5m) wide, the rear wall being squashed so tightly against the back of the rampart that there was no space for an intervallum road. Again, this building was constructed from timber, the floor being raised on stilts above ground level to prevent dampness and vermin. The granary walls had louvred panels at high level to assist with ventilation and the roof would have been covered with shingles for waterproofing. A covered loading bay would have been situated at the east end of the granary to assist in the transfer of grain. The fortlet granary, due to its size, clearly had an important role. Its position alongside the York to Chester road might suggest use as either a transshipment or local distribution centre.

The Stable/Latrine Building - Evidence of a timber structure, 65 feet (20m) x 20 feet (6m) was found adjacent to the rampart in the south-west quarter of the fortlet. Within this area was a circular pit, which, when excavated in 1908, was found to be 7 feet (2.1m) diameter x 18.5 feet (5.64m) deep. It had been dug through the local shale and the excavators reported that the well was lined with timber, as 'the marks of the planks were seen on the shale sides of the well'. Many finds were made in the well including a coin of Hadrian, reticulated leather, two pointed stakes (the so-called *pila muralia*) and a lead lamp holder. During the 1984 excavations the building was again examined and it was found that little remained after Bruton's excavation. Despite the lack of physical evidence to indicate its function, the proximity of water from the well and the fact that this is the lowest area of the fortlet, might suggest that the building served as a latrine block. To substantiate this theory, a drain passing beneath the rampart in this area was discovered during the 1908 excavations, which may have been the outlet from the latrines. The absence of a stable block or store building from the site might equally suggest that the structure contained one or the other or a combination of stable, store and latrine.

The abandonment of the fortlet

It is considered that the abandonment of the fortlet was associated with the building of Hadrian's Wall in the AD 120s. Undoubtedly the dispositions of troops changed and it is thought that the Castleshaw unit may have moved north to assist with the building of Hadrian's new frontier. The finds from both the 1908 and 1984 excavations support this theory. In 1908 the excavators reported, 'taken as a whole, the pottery appears to indicate an occupation of the Castleshaw forts towards the end of the first century, which may have continued in the early years of the second century.' The excavators of 1984 stated 'the finds from Castleshaw suggest the fortlet remained in use until the AD 120s.'

The function of the fortlet

At the conclusion of the 1984 excavations, Greater Manchester Archaeological Unit published their findings in a report, *Castleshaw - The Archaeology of a Roman Fortlet - 1989*. The report devotes much space to discussion relating to the function of the fortlet and includes a comprehensive gazetteer of all the supposed fortlets found in Britain.

Roman fortlets are said to fall into three classes:
a) Barrack fortlet: interior dominated by accommodation and store buildings to house a detachment of troops.
b) Base fortlet: a reduced form of fort housing a dispersed unit. The interior would normally have the core buildings of a standard unit.
c) Commissary fortlet; a supply or control fortlet, the interior being dominated by supply (granaries and stores) and administrative buildings.

It can be argued that Castleshaw 2 could be either a Base or Commissary type. The interior buildings fulfil the requirements of either type. A further possibility is that the fortlet had both a supply and a garrison role. The role of the fortlet at Castleshaw depends upon future exploration increasing our knowledge of the surrounding area. Much work is required in expanding our knowledge of Roman roads, the discovery of watch-towers, signal stations, perhaps marching or practice camps before the true purpose of the fortlet is known.

Plate 29 - The inner and outer ditches at the north gateway. 1984-88

Plate 30 - The main road (via principalis) crossing the fortlet. 1984-88

CHAPTER SIX
Outside the Forts

It was common for Roman forts to have a number of features outside the military enclosure. The civilian settlement *(vicus)* developed around the fort and accommodated the soldiers' families along with the various tradesmen that were required to supply the needs of fort and settlement. All but the most temporary forts would have an external bathhouse and a cemetery. These three features were all found at the adjacent forts of Manchester, Slack and Melandra. It had long been suspected that extra-mural activity (settlement), might have taken place at Castleshaw, even though the site was short-lived and agriculturally, climatically and strategically marginal.

The Civil Settlement

Historic Background

In the winter of 1973, whilst investigating the route of the Roman road, the author and David Chadderton recorded a number of crop marks, visible in melting snow conditions in Daycroft Field. The information was communicated to the Department of Archaeology at the University of Manchester.

In 1984 before to the excavation of the fortlet, a site compound was established in an area to the east of the fort. Whilst constructing a temporary drainage system, evidence of possible building slots and gulleys were found. The date of the remains has not been established. They probably belonged to the fort phase and are related to Roman buildings in the settlement that was built alongside the road leaving the east gate of the fort. As part of the continuing programme of management and research at the site, the Greater Manchester Archaeological Unit undertook an evaluation of extra-mural activity to form a better understanding of the extent of the Roman remains and the function of the site. The project began in 1994, directed by Norman Redhead of the G.M.A.U. and was funded by the landowners, North West Water (now United Utilities).

Exploration

In 1994 two exploratory trenches were excavated opposite the south-west corner of the fortlet defences. The discovery of Roman deposits in one of the trenches led to larger scale investigations in the summers of 1995 and 1996.

The main area of exploration was Daycroft Field, which is situated on the remainder of the level ground to the south of the Roman site. The method of excavation took the form of a series of 3.3 feet (1m) square test pits (TP) set in a 33 foot (10 m) grid across the field. In all, a total of 41 test pits and 5 trenches were investigated in addition to the two trenches dug in 1994. The contents of all the trenches, with the exception of one of those dug in 1994 and a number of the test pits (TP), revealed evidence of Roman occupation as given in the following schedule.

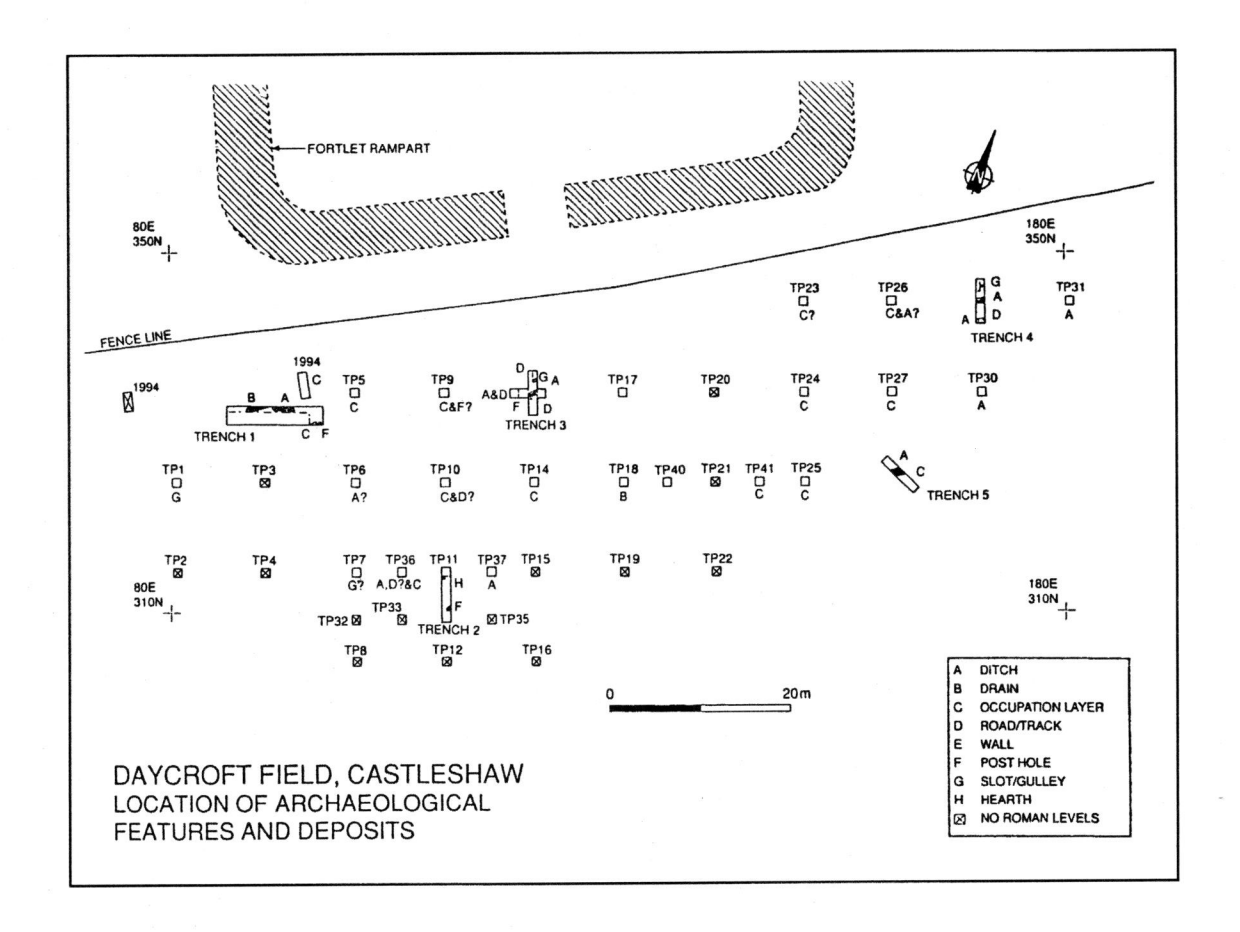

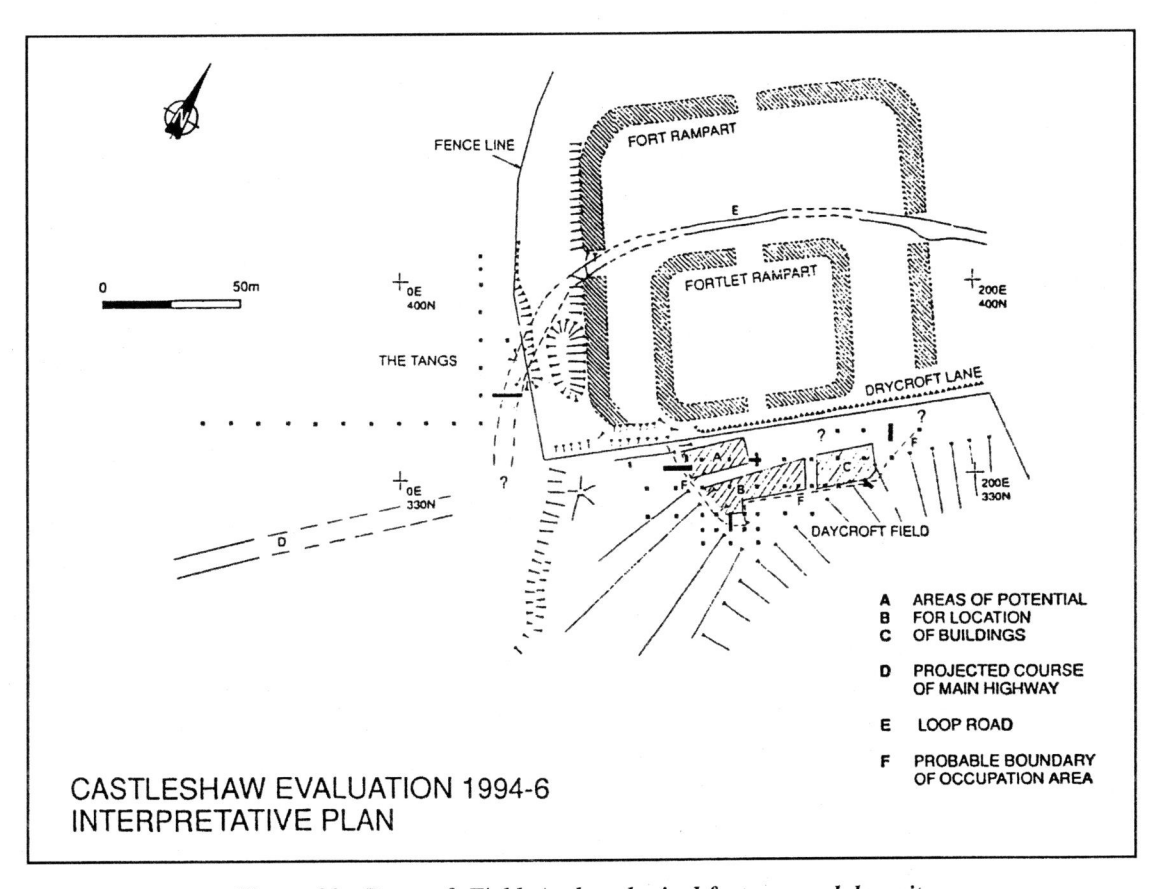

Figure 23 - Daycroft Field. Archaeological features and deposits

1994

Trench E - Roman pottery sherds, amphora, a flagon rim and handle, rusticated grey-ware, burnished ware and tile.

1995-6

Trench 1 - A shallow ditch or hollow way, a stone drain, a boundary ditch, a post-hole and a dwarf stone wall.

Trench 2 - The remains of an oven or hearth.

Trench 3 - The remnants of the major highway (M712), which passed outside the south rampart of the fort. The trench also exposed a section of road that may have been a service road within the vicus, and also a post-hole.

Trench 4 - A road surface 2.6 m. wide with side ditches.

Trench 5 - A ditch and charcoal deposits.

Of the 41 test pits excavated, 15 were barren of Roman deposits. Others revealed remains of roads, ditches, floors, drains and general occupation deposits. The dateable evidence came from test pits 24, 25, 27 and 41, where samian ware pottery was recovered. Test pit 27 produced a sherd from a finely decorated samian vessel of Drag. 37 form.*

The numerous standardised samian vessel forms have been given identification numbers, mostly by an archaeologist named Dragendorff and abbreviated to Drag. (Dr.) Most of the samian ware found in this country was manufactured in Gaul (present day France with some part of northern Germany). One of the commonest forms, the hemispherical bowl with moulded ornamentation on the outside, was Dragendorff's Form 37.

Further investigative work was carried out in the area to the west of the fort known as The Tangs. Of the eleven test pits dug on a line running westwards from the south-west corner of the fort, only two, TP100 and TP101 provided positive evidence of Roman occupation. A second line of test pits was dug on a line parallel to the western rampart of the fort. In addition to the above test pits a trench (Trench 10) was excavated adjacent to the south-west corner of the fort and all evidence of archaeological interest was found to be confined to this area. In Trench 10 and TP100 a dense spread of stones was encountered which was interpreted as the remains of a Roman road linking the main highway (M712) to the western gate of the fort. Other features of interest were confined to a possible building slot in TP115 and post-holes in TP101. It has been suggested that the above features may relate to Roman structures situated besides the link road.

The evidence recovered from the trenches and test pits in Daycroft Field proved the existence of a civil settlement *(vicus)*. The area was not defended in a military manner as no evidence of a substantial ditch or rampart was discovered and in fact, it may not have been formally enclosed. There is some scant evidence of a ragged boundary or fence, partly ditched, enclosing the occupied area. Within the settlement area the presence of buildings are suggested but it is impossible to define their shape or function until a more intensive open area excavation can take place. Daycroft Field has produced evidence of drains, wall foundations, post-holes for buildings and an oven or hearth base. The most positive evidence for buildings within the settlement occurred in Trench 1 where a dwarf stone wall and associated post-hole were revealed. Buildings within Roman settlements were normally individual structures separated by drains and narrow lanes, all features present in Daycroft Field. The buildings within the settlement at

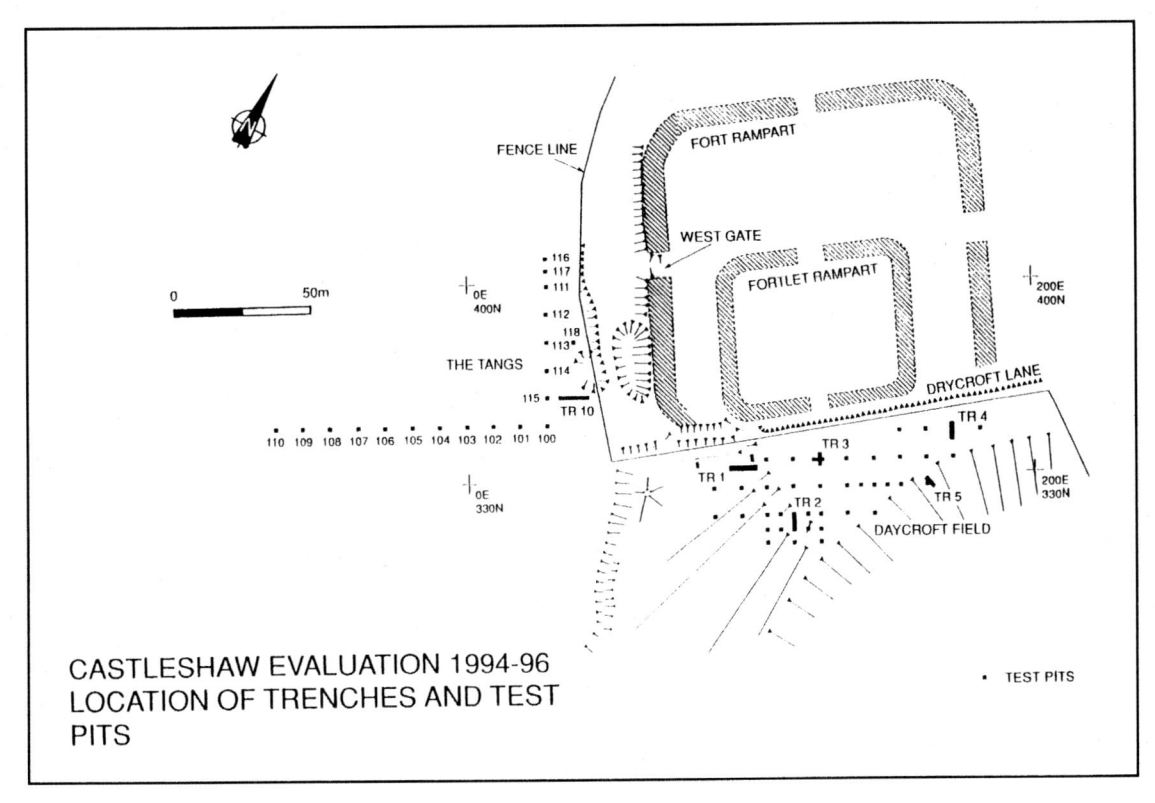

Figure 24 - The Tangs and Daycroft Field

Castleshaw would generally be constructed from timber and have a thatched roof. The stone dwarf wall referred to above may have belonged to an important building, perhaps a small granary within the settlement. The scatter of fragments of samian ware pottery found in TP24, 27, 41 and 25 suggested a potential building roughly measuring 82 feet (25m) x 39 feet (12m), and perhaps occupied by a high status official.

Evidence that the occupants of the settlement at Castleshaw were engaged in agricultural activities was presented during the explorations. Two ditches, which ran out of the settlement area into Daycroft Field, may be Roman allotment divisions or part of a field system. An analysis of the pollen from one of the ditches gave a rare picture of the Roman upland environment indicating a managed, open pastureland.

Whilst the evaluation was of a limited nature, a certain amount of fort activity was identified, but the remains had been either removed or obscured by later occupation. The dateable evidence from the site suggests an early second century occupation, indicating that the settlement was contemporary to the fortlet phase. The civilian occupants of the settlement appear to have been totally dependant on the Roman fortlet. The fortlet was abandoned in cAD120 and archaeological evidence indicates that the settlement was burned and the site cleared about this time. The pollen analysis suggests that following the abandonment of the fortlet the managed pastureland quickly reverted to wilderness.

The Bathhouse

Bathhouses were generally built outside auxiliary forts. They were constructed from stone and tile to minimise the risk of fire and were often sited at a lower level than the fort on a slope down to a nearby stream or river, to ensure a good water supply.

The bathhouse at Castleshaw has not yet been discovered but two sites deserve investigation:

1) A flat platform in Waters Clough below the south rampart of the fort.

    Waters Clough offers an ideal site, a small but level platform next to a stream and below the fort. The streams descending from Standedge would offer an ample water supply and Waters Clough a source of drainage.
    A number of test pits were dug in this area by The Greater Manchester Archaeological Unit in 1998 but proved negative.

2) An area adjacent to the south-west corner of the fort.

    Again, this is an ideal site, lying on falling ground and able to take advantage of the streams descending from Standedge. An aerial photograph taken in 1995 indicates possible Roman activity at this site. It is worth recalling the finds of Roman brick or tile and the dense spread of stones in this area.

Plate 31 - The environs of Castleshaw Roman forts. 1995

The Cemetery

In 450BC, Roman law was embodied in the 'Twelve Tables', of which, table 10 stated that burials had to be outside towns or forts. Livy, the Roman historian who died in 12AD, said that the law of the Twelve Tables was 'the foundation of all public and private law'.

Table 10 covers the laws of burial and it is worth quoting in full.

Table X - Of sacred law

Dead bodies must not be buried or burned within the city.

The wood of a funeral pyre must not be smoothed with the axe.

Not more than three mourners wearing mourning robes, or more than one wearing a purple tunic, may attend a funeral, and not more than ten flute players may be hired.

Women must not disfigure their faces, tear their hair or indulge in excessive wailings.

The bones of a deceased person are not to be collected for the purpose of a second funeral unless he died on the field of battle or in a foreign country.

Slaves' bodies must not be embalmed and drinking bouts, costly besprinkling of the funeral pyre, long garlands and incense boxes are forbidden. However, the deceased is entitled to have placed on his body at the funeral a wreath won by himself or his slaves or horses, or his father may wear it.

No person shall have more than one crier.

Gold must not be buried with the dead, but if teeth are fastened with gold it is not unlawful to bury or burn it with the body.

A funeral pyre or sepulchre must not be placed within sixty feet of another man's house, except with his consent.

Neither a tomb nor its enclosure can be acquired by use.

This law had to be observed throughout the Empire, and therefore by the soldiers in the forts at Castleshaw.

As yet the site of the cemetery at Castleshaw has not been located, but a number of early writers have left clues to its whereabouts:

Some account of a Roman station lately discovered on the borders of Yorkshire
Rev. John Watson - Archaeologia Vol. 1 1770
The places of antiquity near Castleshaw, besides the above military way, are two pieces of ground called the Burying Grounds.

Saddleworth Sketches - Joseph Bradbury 1871
Opposite the village school is a small uneven field, which is locally called 'the burying ground' and where it is supposed the Roman soldiers were buried.

Letter from F.A. Bruton to S. Andrew 1907 (sent during the excavations at Castleshaw) - Samuel Andrew Archive No 55 - Oldham Museum.
The road, so far as we can see, runs out of the fort towards Schofield's barn. In that case it would be making about straight for the Burial Plek would it not. I don't like to theorise but the Romans had a way of burying along the side of their main road.

Excavation of the Roman forts at Castleshaw - First Interim Report 1908
F.A. Bruton
A long lane descending steeply from Bleak Hey Nook and skirting a field known locally as the 'Burial Plek' (the name is yet unexplained) brings us to the village of Castleshaw.

Inhumation and cremation were both practised until c400BC when cremation became the norm. In the 2nd century AD inhumation became popular again. From the above it will be seen that the burials associated with Castleshaw would be both cremation (fort) and inhumation (fortlet).

The literary evidence is suggesting two possible sites for the Roman cemetery:

1) The small, triangular, uneven field on the south side of the road from Bleak Hey Nook, opposite Castleshaw School House.
2) The road referred to by Bruton, in his letter to Andrew in 1907, is the link road that leaves the east gate of the fort. It is shown on the plan that accompanies the excavation reports of 1908 and 1911 and joining the main highway (M712) on the hillside, after passing beneath the now demolished Schofield's Barn. It may well be that the cemetery lay a little to either the north or east of Castleshaw Farm.

Signal Stations

The forts at Castleshaw and the road connecting them to Manchester in the southwest and Slack in the north-east lay within the Roman military zone. In order to facilitate lateral communication it may be that a series of signal stations was built along the line of the Roman road between the forts. The signal stations would be timber towers surrounded by an earth rampart and ditch, the tower being of sufficient height to be in sight of the adjoining towers.

Because of the hilly nature of Saddleworth and because the forts at Castleshaw are situated below the Standedge ridge, careful consideration would have to be given to the sites of such towers. The first location could possibly have been on the summit of High Moor (now destroyed by quarrying). High Moor was the first alignment point used by the Roman surveyors when plotting the line of the Roman road from Manchester to Castleshaw, both of which would be visible from the summit of High Moor. The second location for a signal station could have been at the western end of Standedge (SE00351158), which lies close to the summit of Oldgate Clough, the route of the Roman road. From this point it is possible to see High Moor, Castleshaw forts, north-eastwards towards the next Roman fort at Slack and southwards towards the Roman fort at Melandra, near Glossop. In 1987 the site of a possible signal station at the eastern end of Standedge was reported, but subsequent excavation proved negative.

1 - The Roman road at New Inn Farm, High Moor 1996

2 - The Roman road crossing the Castleshaw Valley 1996

3 - Roman road excavation at New Inn Farm, High Moor 1973   SD975064

4 - Roman road excavation at Causeway Sett, Delph 1975   SD991087

5 - The fortlet hypocaust building 1984-88

6 - The fortlet oven 1984-88

7 - The author's model of Castleshaw Roman fortlet in Saddleworth Museum

8 - The Minerva Intaglio found in 1986

CHAPTER SEVEN
The Finds

Thomas Pecival 1751

Thomas Percival is the first recorded visitor to the Roman forts at Castleshaw. The visit was made when Percival was tracing the route of the Roman road from Manchester to Slack. Whilst he states that he was *'well pleased to find a double Roman camp'* no mention of any artefacts having been recovered from the site was made.

Rev. John Watson 1766

John Watson's account of Castleshaw, made during a visit in 1766, records:-

I was informed on the spot, that coins, beads, pieces of uncommon pots, and bricks, had some time ago been found there; as also an inscription on a stone, which, not being understood, was unfortunately broke and used.
I could meet with nothing of this fort, except a perforated bead of dark green glass, round, and ornamented, such as Pliny calls "Druidis insigne" which yet might belong to some inhabitant of this garrison.

Watson had made the first recorded find at Castleshaw, a blue melon-shaped glass bead. Melon beads are very frequently found on first and second century sites, especially those with a military origin. The finds mentioned are now lost.

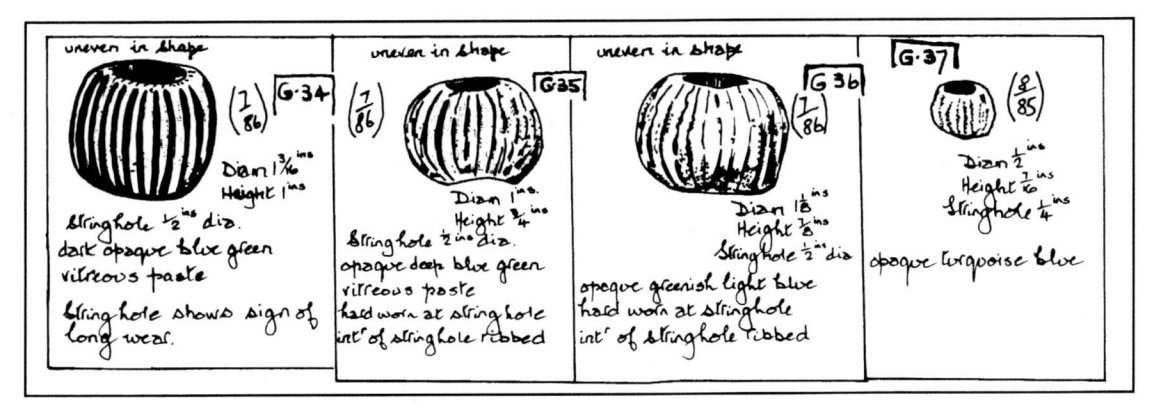

Figure 25 - Glass melon shaped beads; a page from Bruton's record book 1908-09

Finds from the excavations within the Roman fort & fortlet

Ammon Wrigley 1897 and 1898-1907

Wrigley rediscovered the site in 1897 and, along with two friends *'sank trial holes in various parts of the Roman camp area, and were rewarded by finding fragments of Roman tile and pottery'*. The finds records indicate that Wrigley excavated two tile fragments, each bearing an incomplete cohort stamp (the name of the unit that manufactured the tile). Wrigley's excavations also produced a number of Roman coins which are in the Tolson Museum, Huddersfield.

Some of the pottery and tile finds are housed in the Oldham Museum.

George Frederick Buckley 1897

Buckley leased the land at the termination of Wrigley's lease and, in the summer of 1898 *'caused a number of diagonal trenches to be opened near the inner fort'*. The finds recorded included pottery in the form of samian ware and both black and white coarse ware.

The current location of the Buckley finds is unknown.

Bruton 1907-1908

The excavations commenced on the 12th August 1907 and by the close in 1908 an impressive quantity of artefacts had been recovered. The two reports of 1908 and 1911, whilst admirable for their period, concentrated mainly on the finds, and the accompanying plan gave only limited detail of the areas excavated and features located. Whilst the finds book is magnificently illustrated, little information is given of the locations of the artefacts.

The finds book records considerable quantities of:-
1) Pottery - sherds of samian and coarse ware
2) Tile, including a stamped roof tile
3) Mortaria (sherds of general purpose mixing bowls)
4) Amphorae (sherds of large two handled containers for wine and oil)
5) Wood and stone objects
6) Bronze, lead and iron
7) Animal remains
8) Leather
9) Glass

Samian ware - The high quality pottery was in both plain and decorated forms in a bright red glaze. Both forms were well represented by sherds of the many popular patterns and a number of potters' stamps were present.

Coarse ware - The basic every day pottery was found in many forms and shapes including a good selection sherds of jars, beakers, cooking pots, bowls and dishes. Fabric colours ranged from white, grey, buff, black and red.

Tile - Finds included fragments of roof tiles, imbrex tiles (the curved coverings for weathering the edges of the roofing tiles), and box flue tiles (for carrying the hot gases within the walls of the hypocaust building). One of the fragments of roofing tile carried an incomplete stamp (see later chapter dealing with tile stamps).

Mortaria - The heavy rimmed general purpose mixing bowls had pouring spouts and a gritty interior surface to aid mixing. Specialist potters were always involved in their production and a number of the fragments found at Castleshaw had the potters' name-stamps present. One of the name-stamps was of MARINVS who has been identified as Gaius Attius Marinus, working in the first decade of the second century at the kilns at Hartshill/Mancetter in Warwickshire. Mortaria bearing his stamp have been found at other Roman sites in the north of England.

Amphorae - The large two handled containers normally used by the Romans to transport perishable liquids. Two types of amphorae were in use:-

1) The spindle-shaped body type with long handles and a basal spike was used mainly to hold wine imported from Italy.

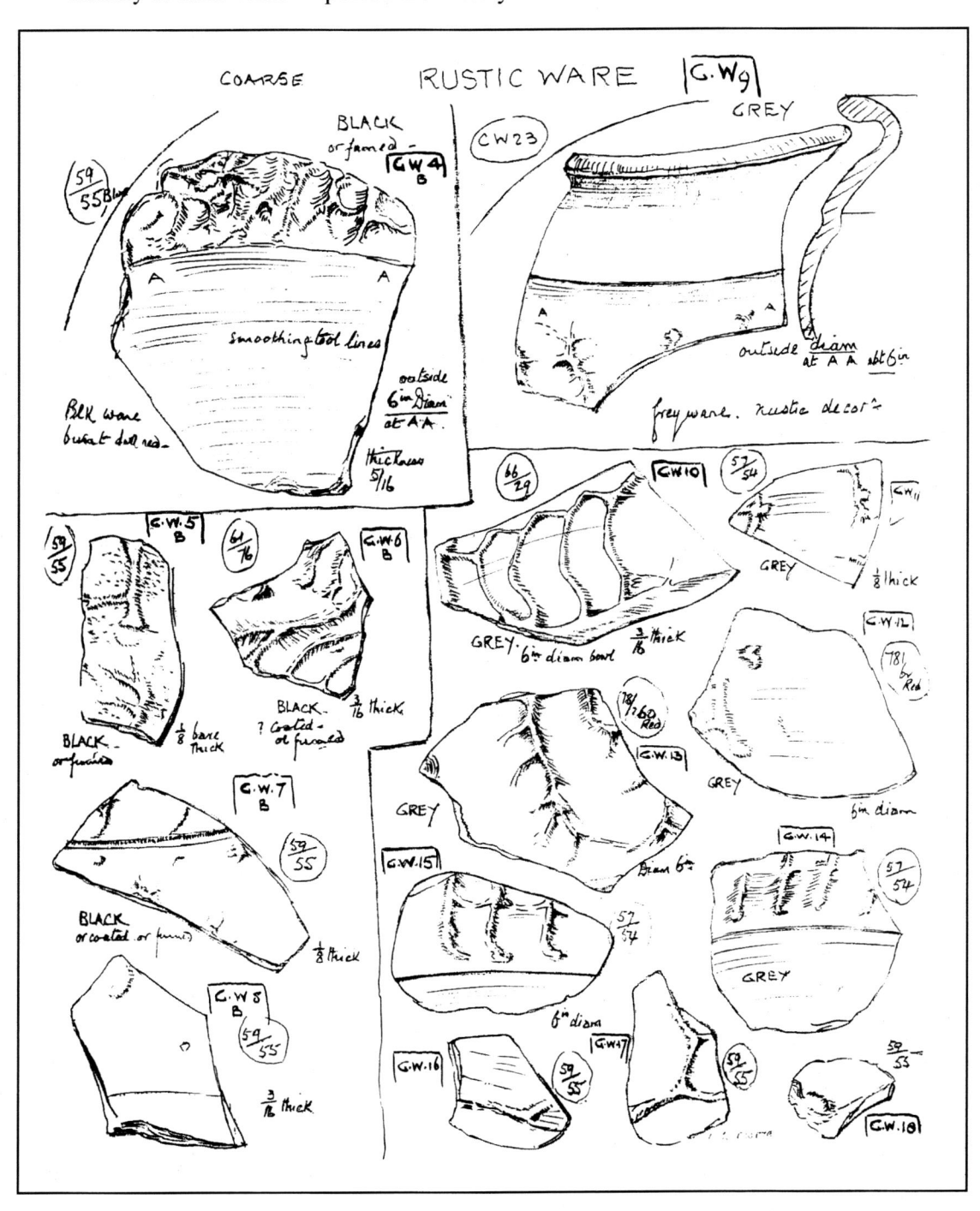

Figure 26 - A page from Bruton's record book. Grey ware pottery

2) The globular variety of amphorae was used to transport olive oil from southern Spain.

As far as can be identified from the fragments found during the 1907-08 excavations, all of the amphorae found at Castleshaw were of the globular variety. One of the fragments displayed part of a stamp indicating that the manufacturer could well have been of southern Spanish origin.

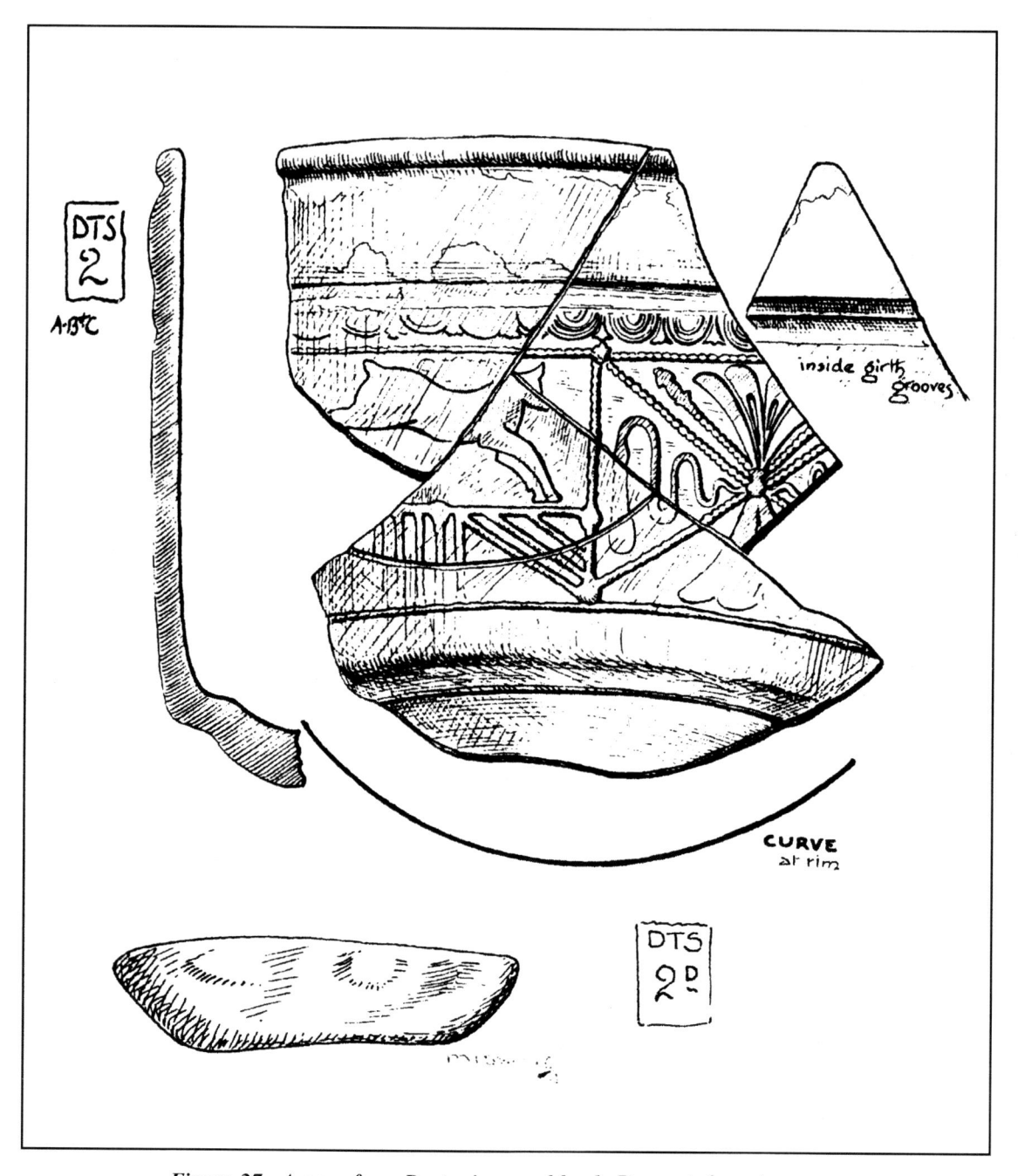

Figure 27 - A page from Bruton's record book. Decorated samian ware

Wood - Various items of wood were found, the most significant being three oak stakes thought to be *pila muralia*.

Pila muralia are wooden stakes, approximately 2.2metres long, with a hand-grip in the centre. Their function was, when planted into the mound of a temporary Roman camp, to form a palisade, the hand-grip facilitating the tying together of the stakes to form a serviceable fence. The Castleshaw stakes were, even when allowing for rotting at the ends, much shorter than the norm, being 4.6 feet (1.4m), 4 feet (1.2m) and 3 feet (0.9m) in length. These would not offer much of a palisade and it may well be that they were

Figure 28 - A temporary barrier or gateway. © *Frank Graham*

used in the construction of a temporary gateway barrier of the type illustrated in 'The Outpost Forts of Hadrian's Wall' by R. Embleton. (see figure 28). Other finds included post ends, the pommel from a Roman dagger and two pieces of wood, very suggestive of having been part of an archer's bow.

Stone - Fragments of several millstones were found of both Roman and beehive form. The site also yielded a great number of small whetstones (shaped stones for giving sharp edges to cutting tools), some possibly not Roman. In the early 19th century, Castleshaw village was the headquarters of the 'Swipper' Scythesmen, who formed the famous 'Lightfleet of Castleshaw'. They were, according to Ammon Wrigley, a band of men who travelled around the valley mowing the fields.

Bronze - Various small items were found including the top half of a small bell, a fragment of the bow of a fibula (a decorative brooch of safety-pin form) and pieces that may well represent strap tags and buttons.

Lead - A leaden lamp-holder was found in the well of the fortlet (Castleshaw 2). It was of a common pattern and a similar one was found at Melandra Castle Roman fort during the 1905 excavations. Pottery fragments in red ware fabric, of similar lamp-holders, were found near the well. Other finds included a number of spindle-whorls, (the small fly-wheel mounted on a spindle to steady its motion whilst twisting fibres of wool into thread for spinning) and various items of unrecognisable sheet lead.

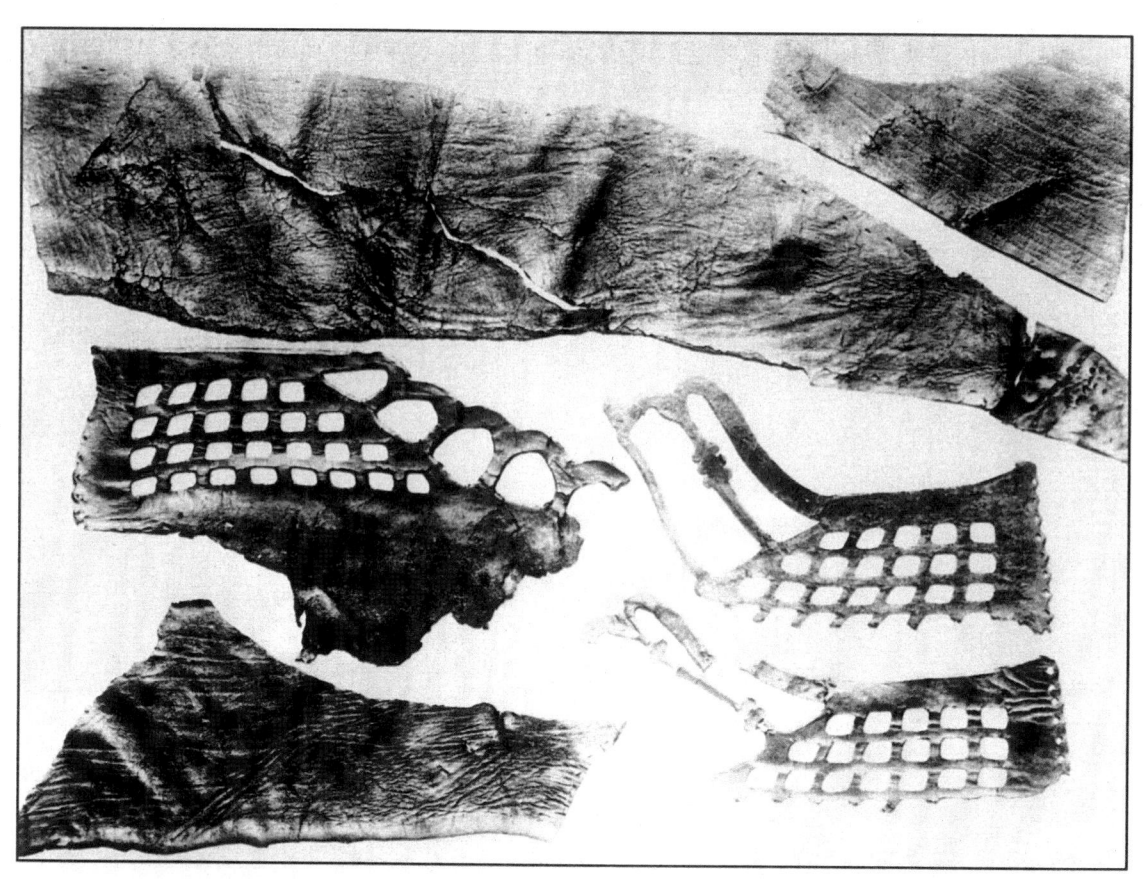

Plate 32 - The uppers of Roman shoes and fragments of plain leather found in the fortlet well.

Plate 33 - Necks of white ware jugs found at Castleshaw fortlet.

Photographs from the Bruton excavations of 1908-09

Plate 34 - Potters' stamps on rims of mortaria found at Castleshaw Roman fortlet

Plate 35 - A fragment of a samian bowl, shape Drag. No. 29

Photographs from the Bruton excavations of 1908-09

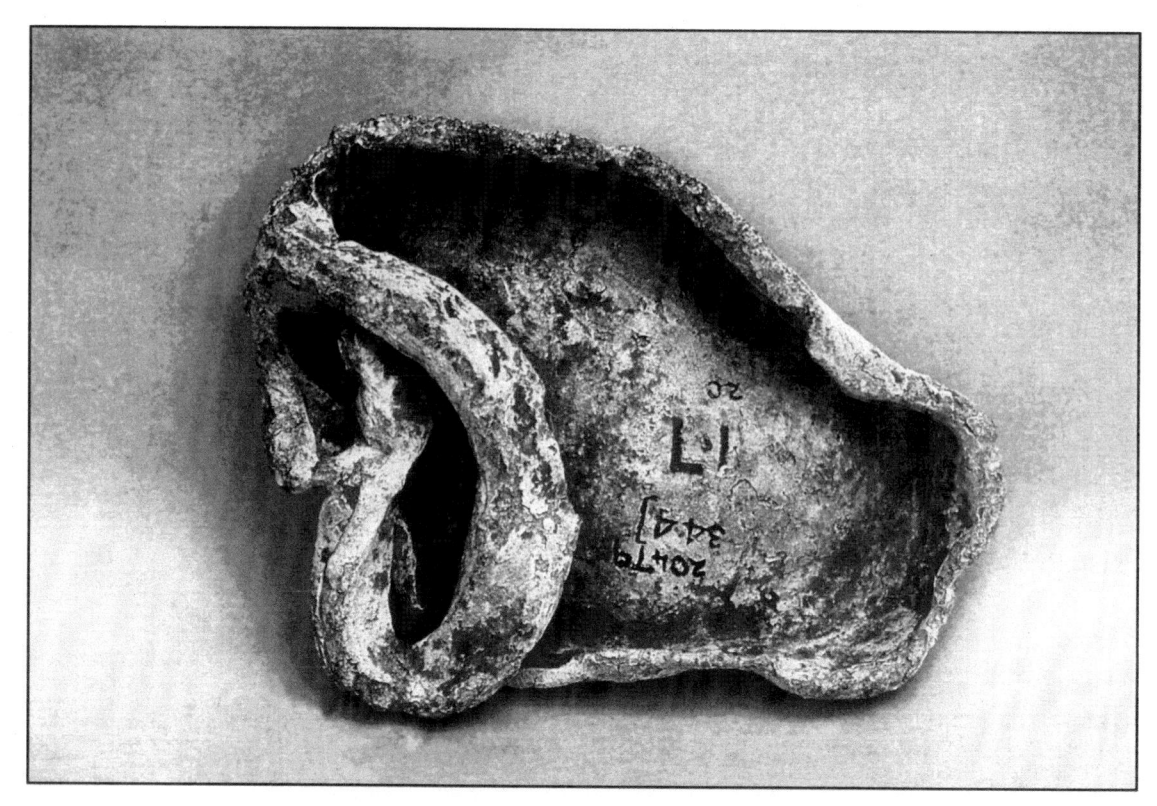

Plate 36 - The lead lamp-holder recovered from the pit or well.

Iron - A numbers of items of corroded iron were found. Some were probably nails whilst others were thought to be the remains of daggers and sword blades.

Animal remains - Mainly teeth and small bones from oxen and horses.

Leather - The well, when excavated, produced eight items of leather. Four of these were the remains of the 'uppers' from Roman sandals; the remaining items were fragments of plain leather.

Glass - Considering that the site was only partially excavated, a considerable number of blue melon-shaped beads were found. Various pieces of blue/green, ribbed glass belonging to pillar moulded bowls, a fragment from a colourless glass beaker, the neck and rim of a blue/green conical flask or jug, a number of pieces from a blue/green square bottle which had a base design of four concentric circular mouldings, and very small fragments of window glass.

The finds together with the illustrated finds book are housed in The Manchester Museum.

Finds from the excavations within the Roman fort
Manchester University Training Excavations 1957-64

Thompson's report of 1967 remarked that 'no striking small finds were recovered from the excavations'.

The finds book does however, record the following;

Coins - Two denarius from a small pit in trench 20 (see later chapter dealing with coin finds).

Bronze - An acorn-shaped finial and a bronze thimble.

Lead - Two circular items of lead were recovered; one may have been a spindle-whorl.

Glass -
1) Five fragments, or complete melon beads. One was in green paste and the remainder were dark blue and glazed.
2) A plano-convex counter in black paste.
3) A fragment of a pale green ring, possibly from a pendant.
4) Various pieces from square green glass bottles with cylindrical necks and reeded handles.

Pottery -
1) Coarse ware - a representative selection of rims from jars and bowls in fabric colours of red, orange, buff, white, grey and black.
2) Mortaria - various fragments were found and potters' stamps were present on two of the rims.
   a) MORICAMVLV - thirty-five stamps of the potter Moricamulus are known from England and Wales. It is known that he was working in the Watling Street area between St Albans and London. c. AD75 - 100.
   b) S] OLLVS - seventy stamps are known from Britain and the Castleshaw find is one of three known dies. The potter worked in the same general area as Moricamulus; the suggested date from evidence found in Scotland and at St. Albans was c. AD 70 - 100.
3) Amphora - six fragments of buff coloured amphora.
4) Samian ware - one fragment of a rim, very worn with the remains of a pattern faintly visible.
5) Iron - a number of items of iron were found together with the remains of forty nails.

A final feature of note was the prehistoric pit found in the south-west edge of trench 6, it was cut into the closely packed flaggy gritstone to a depth of 1.2 feet (380mm) and was 1.8 feet (535mm) in diameter. The pit was filled with a clean orange-brown soil with occasional charcoal fragments and closely packed Beaker sherds representing at least five vessels.

The finds together with the finds book are housed in the Manchester Museum.

Finds from the excavations within the Roman fortlet
The Greater Manchester Archaeological Unit 1984-88

In 1985, on granting permission for work to be carried out on the Roman fortlet, the Department of the Environment restricted excavation to that required to return the monument to its appearance prior to the 1907 excavations. Excavation was allowed in the two gateways, several sections across the ditch system and a reinvestigation of previous work in the interior of the fortlet. This meant that the large majority of the artefacts found were unstratified, coming from the ploughsoil, spoil heaps and the backfill in the old excavation trenches. The stratified finds came mainly from the ditches, the base of the fortlet rampart and the features sealed by the rampart. The excavations produced a remarkable number of artefacts considering the limitations of the work that was allowed to take place.

Samian ware - Many sherds were recovered in both plain and decorated forms. Both forms were well represented by the patterns that are found at many other British sites of this period, the decorated forms representing 60% of the total.

Coarse ware - The pottery found under this general heading included an extensive selection of both form and colour. Forms covered the normal range of jars, beakers, bowls and dishes. Fabric colours ranged from black, grey, red, orange and cream. Included in this class of pottery are the mixing bowls (mortaria) and the storage vessels (amphora). One of the mortaria sherds carried the potter's mark VSTC and, on a sherd of amphora, the mark SLP

Tile - Recovered were large quantities of broken red and orange roofing tiles and buff coloured box flue tiles. This material came from the area around the small hypocaust building. The stacks of red tiles *(pilae)*, which supported the floor, were removed and deposited in Oldham Museum. A fragment of roofing tile bore an incomplete maker's stamp. (see later chapter dealing with tile stamps)

Glass - Some items of blue or green glass were recovered along with twenty-four melon shaped beads made from either blue or turquoise glass paste.

Plate 37 - Samian ware pottery found during the 1984-88 excavations.

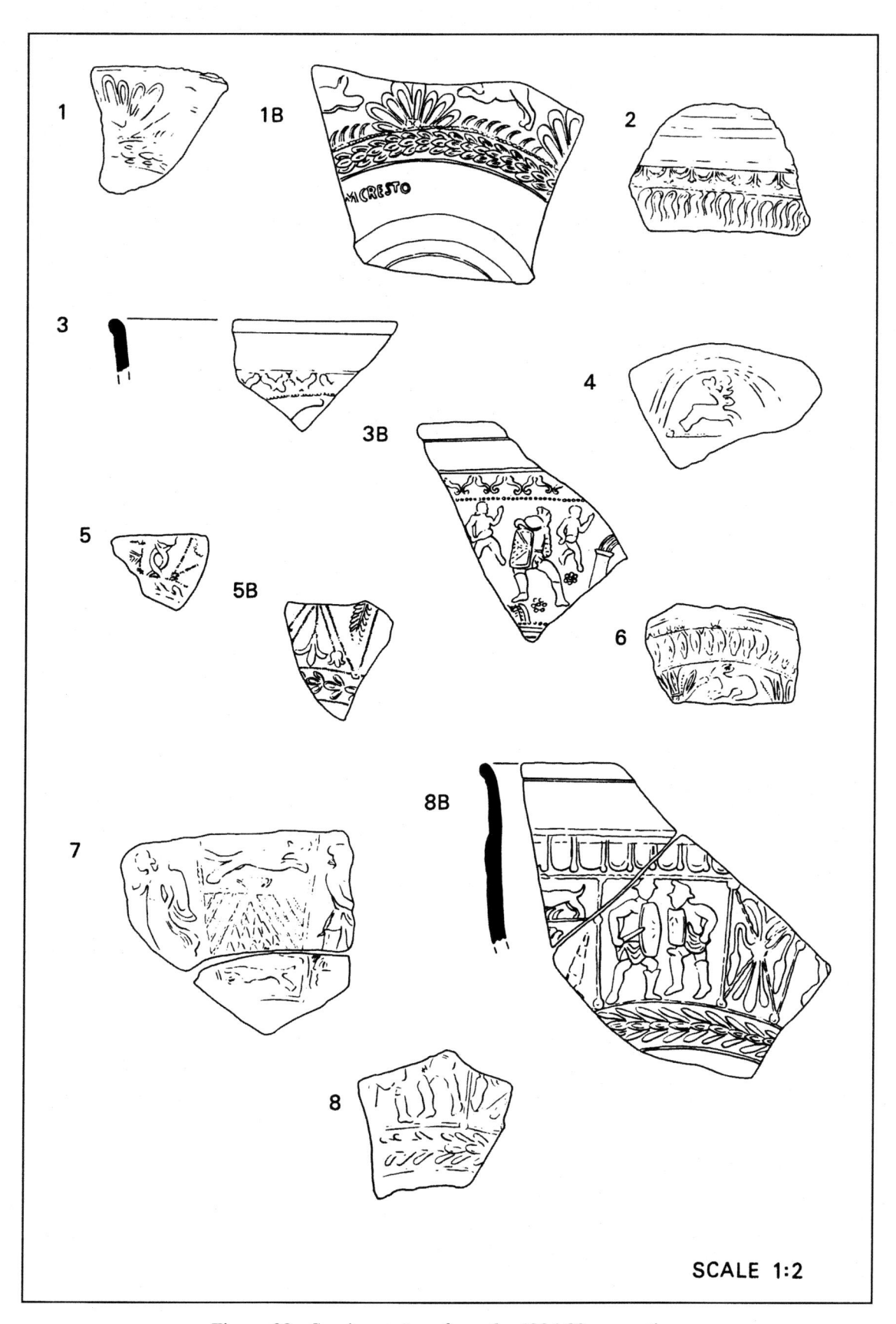

Figure 29 - Samian pottery from the 1984-88 excavations

Iron - Large quantities of nails were discovered, sometimes in the same context as charcoal, leading to the conclusion that the nails and charcoal were all that remained of the dismantled fortlet, which was burnt before the Roman detachment moved on. Many lumps of corroded iron were found along with hobnails from the soldiers' boots.

Bronze - A small collection of bronze items were recovered, one perhaps being the remains of a small bronze bell.

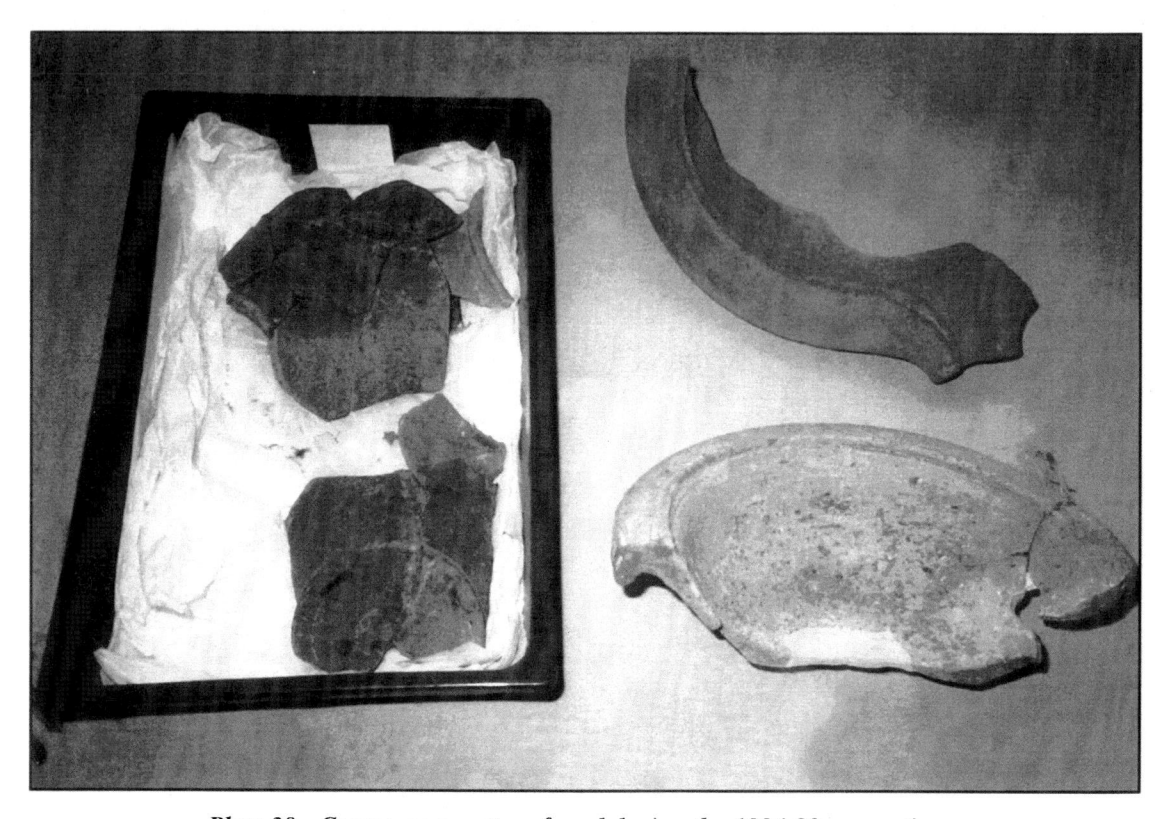

Plate 38 - Coarse ware pottery found during the 1984-88 excavations.

Gaming counters - Thirteen small discs of opaque glass or frit were found during the excavations. Made by pouring the molten material onto a flat surface, they varied from 0.51 inches (13mm) to 0.7 inches (18mm) in diameter and on average 0.23 inches (6mm) high, they were flat based and convex above. They were coloured both white and black, and plain in design. The coloured glass counters were called *calculi, latrones, or milites* and were used for the game *ludus latrunculorum* - the 'soldiers' game'. This was played on a squared board, several of which are known from military sites but none has been found to date at Castleshaw.

Lead - Various items of lead, generally difficult to identify, but one item, a lead dice, could possibly be of Roman date. Dice *(tesserae, tessellae)*, identical to the modern, have been found in sufficient numbers to prove that Roman Britain shared in the general passion for dice playing. Usually made from bone, occasional examples in ivory and lead are also known from Roman sites.

Intaglio - This is a gemstone, with an incised carving, normally mounted in a signet ring. The stone recovered at Castleshaw was oval in shape, 0.55 inches (14mm) x 0.43 inches (11mm) x 0.078 inches (2mm) thick, with a bevelled edge. The intaglio was made from carnelian *(a crypto-crystalline variety of quartz)*, reddish white in colour and depicting Minerva, the Roman goddess of wisdom, standing facing to the right. She holds a spear vertically in her right hand and carries a drape over her left arm. On her head is a plumed helmet, and a shield lies at her feet. This style of gemstone is thought to date to cAD75-85.

Daub - This is clay smeared on to some rigid structure, usually of interwoven twigs (wattle) to exclude draughts and give a smooth finish. It rarely survives unless accidentally baked. The fact that daub was found at Castleshaw gives a clue as to the construction of some of the buildings and to the presumption that the Romans burnt the buildings before they evacuated the fortlet.

Stone - Amongst the stone items found during the excavations were three quern stones (stones used for grinding corn) of Roman date. Two were made from lava stone, an imported material, and the third from millstone grit, a local material found adjacent to the site.

Miscellaneous finds - During the excavations items of bone, slag, coal and chalk were recovered.

All the finds and record cards are housed in the Oldham Museum.

Finds from the excavations within the Civil Settlement
The Greater Manchester Archaeological Unit 1994-96

The excavations in Daycroft Field and The Tangs previously reported, produced a number of finds. The most important of these was the samian ware, which gave the site an approximate date of occupancy.

Samian Ware - Of the samian ware recovered, all was very worn and the distinctive red slip coating surviving on only a few of the sherds. The shape of some of the bowls could be identified (i.e. Drag 37), as could some fragmentary decorations. The samian ware was probably imported from the Central Gaulish potteries where manufacturing was centred at Les Martres-de-Veyre (c AD100-125). A sherd of decorated samian ware (form Drag. 37) was recovered from TP 27 during the 1995 excavations. It is in the style of an anonymous Trajanic potter known only as 'The Potter of the Rossette', a name based on the decorative details of the raised reliefs on the external surface of the vessel.

Coarse Ware - A total of 207 sherds of coarseware pottery were recovered during the excavations. Some of the forms could be identified as fragments of dishes, jars, and flagons. The vessels and fabrics compare with the Flavian / Trajanic material from the Manchester and Melandra vicus areas.

Glass - Of the 34 items of glass recovered, 14 were of Roman date and could be identified as fragments from a tubular rimmed jar and common domestic vessels. All were in use from the mid first to the late third century A.D.

Metalwork - The metalwork recovered was badly corroded and apart from nails, only two other identifiable objects were recovered; a decorative bronze terminal and half of an iron strap hinge.

The finds and record cards are housed in the Oldham Museum.

The Prehistoric finds from the site of the Roman forts

Whitaker's *History of Manchester 1771*, when discussing the Roman fort at Castleshaw, records that *'within one or two fields from it was lately discovered a brazen Celt, hollow in the blade, and carrying a loop at the head'*. The object that Whitaker describes is a Bronze Age looped and socketed axe.

The Second Interim Report of the excavation of the Roman forts, 1911, by F.A. Bruton, recorded the find of a small round flint scraper, probably dating to the Bronze Age.

In the 1957-64 excavations, a pit discovered beneath the floor of the fort was found to contain one hundred and twenty two sherds of Beaker pottery dating from the Bronze Age.

The 1984-88 excavations in the fortlet area produced forty-eight items of flint. The majority of the flints had evidence of worked edges and were mainly from the Mesolithic period. They did however include a Neolithic leaf shaped arrowhead and a Bronze Age barbed and tanged arrowhead.

The finds from the 1911 and the 1957-64 excavations are housed in the Manchester Museum.

The finds from the 1984-88 excavations are housed in the Oldham Museum.

Miscellaneous Roman finds from the Saddleworth area

Lominot, Colne Valley. SE 010125
I.R. Richmond recorded in *Huddersfield in Roman Times (page 83)* that 'a scrap of grey pottery from Lominot seems good evidence for an occupation of this spot near the Roman road between AD80 and AD120'.

Hunters Hill, Delph. SE 002090
The excavation of a Bronze Age round barrow, in 1974, on a ridge over looking the Roman forts, produced, amongst the finds, a fragment of a Roman unguent bottle, greenish in colour and similar in shape to one found at the Roman forts in 1909.

CHAPTER EIGHT
Roman Coins from Saddleworth

Although it has two Roman forts and five miles of well-documented Roman road, Saddleworth has yielded only twenty-two Roman coins to date, plus two more from just outside the boundaries.

1) Coins found in the Roman forts at Castleshaw

Ammon Wrigley Excavations. 1897-1907
F.W. Chadderton, Ammon Wrigley, Arthur Settle and Percy Winterbottom found three silver coins at the forts in 1898. The coins were retained by Chadderton and are now in the Tolson Museum

HADRIAN (AD117-138)	*Silver Denarius*
SABINA, wife of Hadrian (AD117-138)	*Silver Denarius*
LUCIVS VERVS (161-169)	*Silver Denarius*

In May 1899 Ammon Wrigley contributed an article relating to his excavations at Castleshaw, to the Yorkshire Weekly Post in which he listed his finds to date, including a further coin.

VESPASIAN (AD69-79)   *Silver Denarius*

F.A. Bruton Excavations. 1908-11
Castleshaw underwent extensive excavation at the beginning of the last century. In his final report, published in 1911, Bruton gave the following list of coins.

L. RUBRIVS DOSSENVS (c. 87 BC)	*Silver*
TRAJAN (AD 98-118)	*First Brass, illegible*
TRAJAN (AD 98-118)	*First Brass, illegible*
HADRIAN (AD117-138)	*First Brass*

Manchester University Excavations. 1957-64
In 1957 Manchester University began a series of training excavations. F.H. Thompson, in his final excavation report, listed two coins.

NERO (AD 63-68)	*Silver Denarius*
REPUBLICAN	*Silver Denarius - virtually illegible*

Coins from the 1908-11 and the 1957-64 excavations are currently housed in the Manchester Museum.

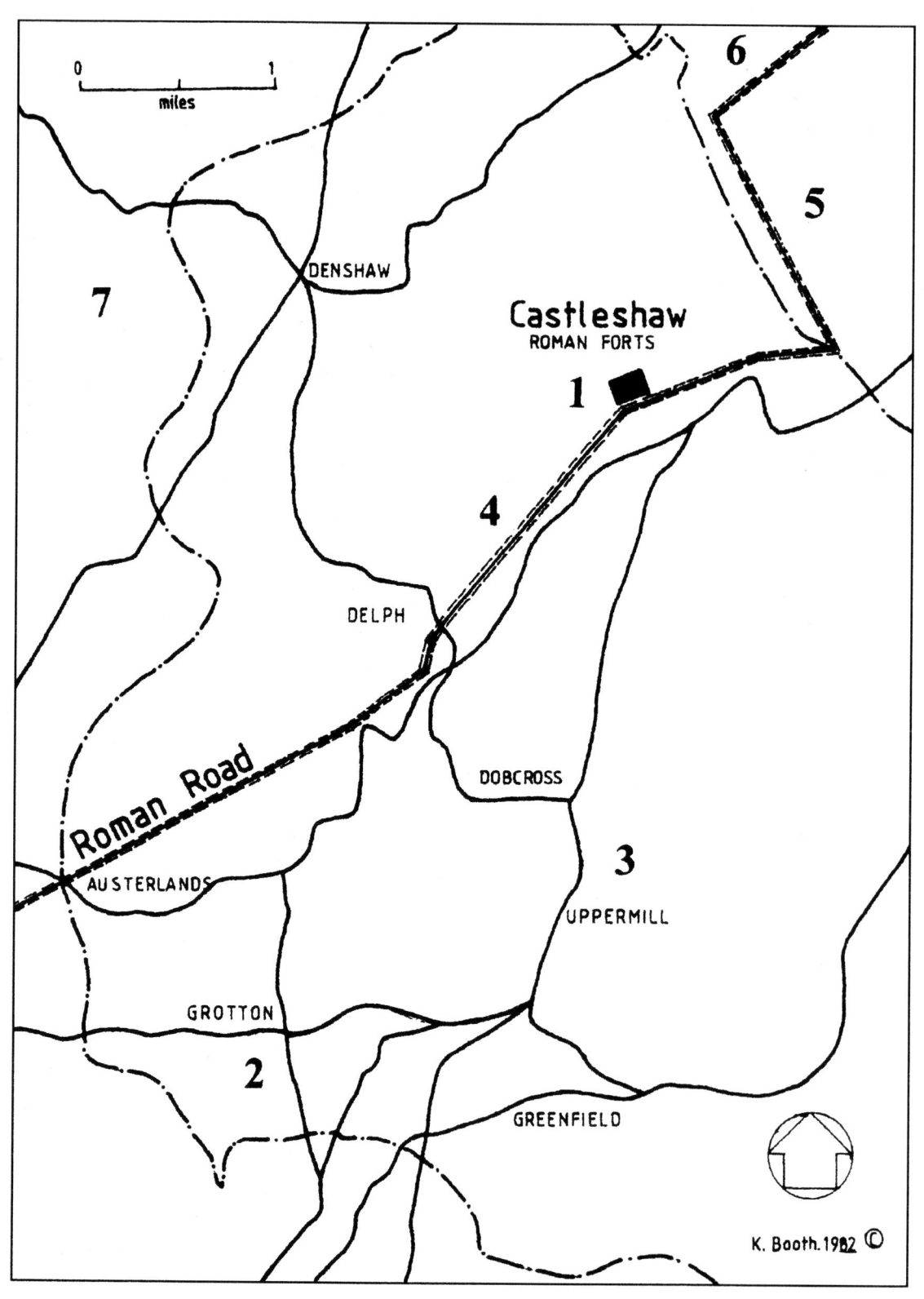

Figure 30 - Roman coin finds in Saddleworth

Greater Manchester Archaeological Unit Excavations. 1984-88
The nine coins found during the above excavations had all suffered badly in the soil, with the result that most show advanced corrosion, and many are fragile or already in fragments. One in fact was little more than an impression in the soil.

REPUBLICAN　　　　　　　　　　*Silver Denarius*
REPUBLICAN　　　　　　　　　　*Silver Denarius 32-31BC*
VESPASIAN　　　　　　　　　　　*Silver Denarius 75 AD*
VESPASIAN　　　　　　　　　　　*Silver Denarius 69-79AD*
VESPASIAN　　　　　　　　　　　*Brass Sestertius 77-78AD*

Only a small fragment of this coin survived, and identification is based on a fine imprint left in the soil.

VESPASIAN　　　　　　　　　　　*Copper As 69-79AD*
VESPASIAN　　　　　　　　　　　*Copper As 69-79AD*
DOMITIAN　　　　　　　　　　　 *Copper As 81-96AD*
FLAVIAN?　　　　　　　　　　　 *Copper As 69-79AD*

Coins from the 1984-88 excavations are currently housed in the Oldham Museum.

Coins found outside the Roman forts

2) Thornlee Hall, Grotton
Found in a piggery by Mr H.H. Potts in 1875.

DOMITIAN (AD81-96)　　　　　　*Copper As*

Coin in private hands

3) Uppermill
Found near Ballgrove by Mr. J.F. Buckley in 1930.

PROBVS (AD276-282)　　　　　　*Billon Tetradrachm*

Coin in private hands.

4) Castleshaw Valley

DIOCLETIAN (AD284-305)

Coin in the Oldham Museum.

5) Millstone Edge
The find of a Roman coin is noted on the record sheets in Saddleworth Museum.

6) Lominot, Colne Valley.

CARACALLA (AD211-217)

Coin in the Tolson Museum, Huddersfield.

7) Crow Knowl, Crompton
Found by Mr. G. Radford of Denshaw.

ANTONINUS PIUS (AD138-161)   *Third Brass, illegible*

Coin was in the Tolson Museum, now lost.

The overall chronological distribution of the coins is as follows:

Issuer	From the Forts	Others	Total	
Republican (up to 31BC)	4		4	
Nero (54-68AD)	1		1	
Vespasian (69-79AD)	6		6	
Domitian (81-96AD)	1	1	2	**(1)**
Flavian (69-96AD)	1		2	
Trajan (98-117AD)	2		2	
Hadrian (117-138)	2		2	**(2)**
Sabina (117-138AD), Wife of Hadrian	1			
Antonius Pius (138-161AD)		1	1	
Lucius Verus (161-169AD)	1		1	
Caracalla (211-217AD)		1	1	
Probus (276-282AD)		1	1	
Diocletian (284-305AD)		1	1	
Total	19	5	24	

(1) Fort phase cAD79 - AD90
(2) Fortlet phase cAD105 - AD120

For readers unfamiliar with the Roman coinage system the following reference section is included at this juncture before discussion of the coins and their significance takes place.

Roman Currency System

1 Aureus (Gold)	= 25 Denarii
1 Denarius (Silver)	= 4 Sestertii
1 Sestertius (Orichalcum)	= 2 Dupondii
1 Dupondius (Orichalcum)	= 2 Asses
1 As (Copper)	= 2 Semisses
1 Semis (Copper)	= 2 Quadrantes (Copper)

Metals

Symbols in use

AV = Gold
AR = Silver
AE = Brass 1st, 2nd or 3rd

Augustus made an important change when he introduced a system whereby some coins were struck in *orichalcum* (4parts of copper to one part of zinc), instead of bronze (copper, tin and lead), and other coins struck in copper *aes* (see above).

Imperial bronze coinage bearing the letters **S***(enatus)* **C***(onsulto)* comprised the *sestertius* (First Brass) and the *dupondius* (Second Brass). Two copper coins of the period were the *as* and the *quadrans*, the *as* was indiscriminately grouped with the *dupondius* as a Second Brass and the *quadrans* were known as Third Brasses.

Only the coins that have derived from controlled excavations at the Roman forts are considered in the following discussion. Random finds, whilst of general interest, are of little use in reviewing the evidence provided by the Roman coins found at Castleshaw and in assessing the contribution they make to our understanding of the site.

The random finds may help to give clues to the general picture of Roman Saddleworth, for example the coin found at Lominot close to the route of the Roman road. Others coins give no clues to the significance of the location where found and may have been more recent losses.

Values of the Roman coins found at Castleshaw

Issuer	Denarii	Sestertii	Asses
Republican	4		
Nero	1		
Vespasian	3	1	2
Domitian			1
Flavian			1
Trajan		2	
Hadrian	1	1	
Sabina	1		
Lucius Verus	1		
Totals	11	4	4

Discussion

In 1993, Dr. David Shotter from the University of Lancaster reviewed the Roman coins from Castleshaw in an article published in the Manchester Archaeological Bulletin Vol. 8. The author is indebted to Dr. Shotter for permission to reproduce the following extracts from his paper.

Some observations may be made on the distribution of Roman coins-

First, The proportion of republican **denarii** in the sample is notable at c36%; these coins remained in general circulation in Britain until late in Trajan's reign or early in Hadrian's. Trajan's recall of old silver coinage around A.D.107 (Dio Cassius LXVIII. 15,3) resulted in the disappearance from circulation of most pre-Neronian **denarii**, with the exception of the legionary issues of Marcus Antonius, which escaped the recall due to the erroneous view that their silver content was inferior; these coins in fact remained in circulation until the first half of the third century. The substantial presence of republican **denarii** in this sample, combined with the near-absence of post-Hadrianic issues, suggest that activity at Castleshaw did not outlast the early years of Hadrian's reign. No conclusion however, can be drawn from the presence of republican **denarii** concerning the commencement of occupation.

Secondly, as noted earlier, the presence of a coin of Lucius Verus should not be taken to indicate necessarily an extension of occupation into the Antonine period. Rather, it and the other two **denarii** found in 1898 were possibly part of a hoard. Hoards terminating with coins of Marcus Aurelius or Lucius Verus are common in north-west England, and a parallel to this small group exists in that found at Ribchester in 1978 (Shotter 1990, 144f). There is in any case no indication of the precise findspot of the 1898 **denarii**.

Thirdly, Flavian and pre-Flavian coins make up two-thirds of the sample. This leaves little doubt that the site was established at least as early as the governorship of Agricola (77-83AD), the absence, however, of pre-Flavian aes issues makes it unlikely that the foundation was earlier than this. The condition of the coins of Vespasian is so poor that it is seldom possible to date them to a precise year within the reign. In fact, the only datable coins of Vespasian are little-worn issues of AD75 and 77-78. On balance, therefore, an Agricolan foundation appears more likely, particularly in view of the pottery evidence (Webster 1989, 69ff).

Fourthly, the low showing of Domitian's coins is remarkable, suggesting a factor in the occupation effecting the circulation of these coins. The most likely such factor is a break in activity in the late 80s or 90s, perhaps coinciding with the post-Agricolan withdrawal from northern Scotland around AD 87. The low showing of Domitian's coins, together with the absence of Nerva's, tends to indicate that occupation was not resumed before the latest years of the first century.

Fifthly, the number of Trajanic coins is small by comparison with Flavian issues. On a larger sample, a suitable parallel would appear to be provided by Ribchester. In this case, the explanation generally accepted, is a break in activity early in Hadrian's reign on the ground that Trajan's coins would otherwise have continued to circulate freely in the reign of his successor. Movements in connection with the construction of the Hadrianic frontier provide an obvious context. In the case of Castleshaw, the low showing of Trajanic coins, together with the two Hadrianic coins recorded from the site, serves to show that this early Hadrianic break proved to be permanent.

Thus, with regard to chronology, although it is not possible to use the coin evidence to differentiate between the two separate phases both of the fort and fortlet, the main distinction between the fort and fortlet can be observed:

The fort phases - early Flavian (probably Agricolan) to the late 80s or early 90s.

The fortlet phases - late Flavian or early Trajanic to early Hadrianic.

Finally, a point may be made concerning the denominational makeup of the coins from Castleshaw. Of the nineteen coins, eleven (58%) are **denarii**. Even if we exclude the four **denarii** found in 1898, the proportion of **denarii** is still as high as 37%. It may reasonably be suggested that this is a reflection of the nature of the manning of the site, since different types of unit - legionary, auxiliary cavalry, auxiliary infantry - were paid in different denominations. The only direct evidence for a unit of the Roman army at Castleshaw consists of the stamped tiles of **Cohors III Breucorum** (Redhead 1989). The substantial proportion of **denarii** suggests the presence at Castleshaw at some stage either of a unit paid at a higher rate (perhaps legionaries) or of more highly paid officials, perhaps concerned with supply and distribution activities based at the site.

Thus, it can be seen that whilst the evidence of coin loss cannot by itself solve any of the problems of occupation at Castleshaw, it can make a constructive contribution to a discussion, which calls upon all of the available evidence.

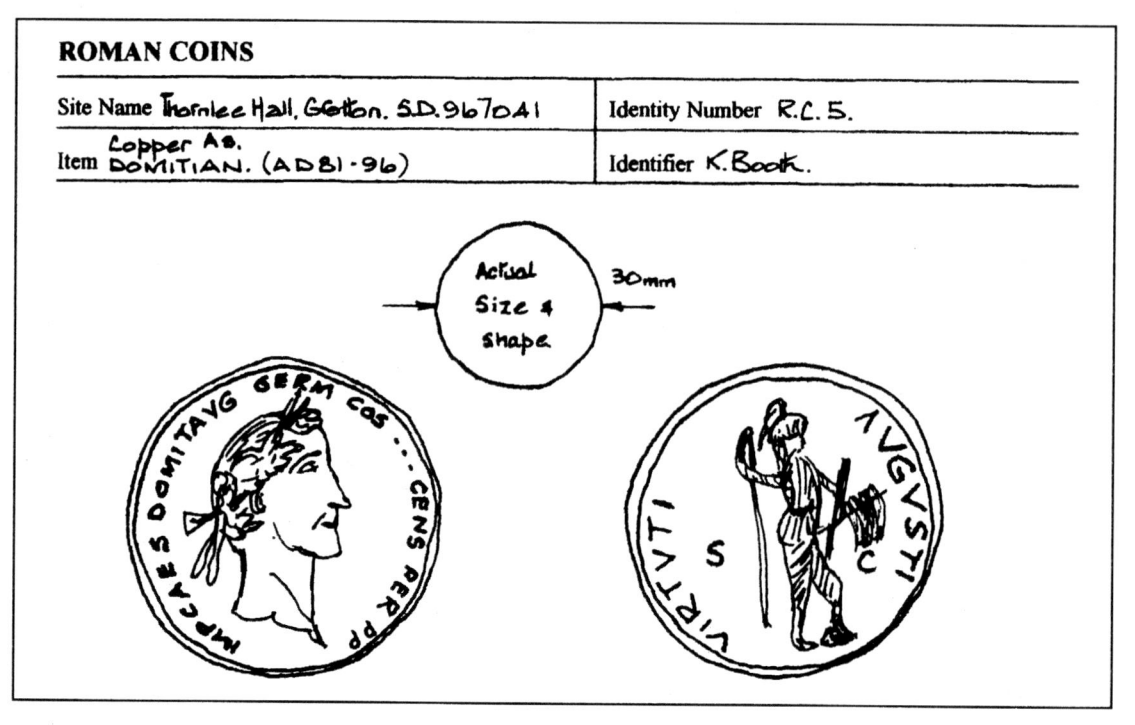

Figure 31 - The Roman coin from Thornlee Hall, Grotton. (the author's record card)

Figure 32 - A Roman coin found during the 1908-09 excavations

Plate 39 - The Billon Tetradrachm of the emperor Probus (AD276-282). Dark copper and 18mm diameter. Found at Ball Grove, Uppermill.

CHAPTER NINE
The Tile Stamps from Castleshaw

The Romans introduced into Britain their long established practice of setting up inscribed stones in the form of religious dedications, tombstones, milestones, and as records of building work. They also had a tradition of inscribing weapons, tools, domestic utensils, and ingots of metal and so forth with the name of the owner. Many of the domestic utensils, pottery, bricks and tiles, were often stamped with the name of the maker or makers. The value of Roman inscriptions as historical material is immense. They are contemporary and authoritative documents whose text is free from corruption, and are one of the most important single sources for the history and organisation of the Roman Empire.

The Roman forts at Castleshaw have not produced any inscriptions on stone. However pottery finds, mainly samian ware and mortaria have been found inscribed with the name of the potters involved in the manufacture. During the various excavations that have taken place at Castleshaw, four fragments of stamped tile have been recovered. It has been scientifically established by analysis, that the tiles were manufactured at the Roman tilery in Grimscar Wood, near Huddersfield (Grid. Ref. SE 131191).

The site at Grimscar, first discovered in 1590 is described in a sixteenth century diary preserved among the Dodsworth Manuscripts in the Bodleian Library, Oxford. The colliers, who discovered the tile kiln whilst digging a pit in which to burn charcoal, recovered a large tile bearing the inscription COHIIIIBRE. Excavations at Grimscar in 1955-56 revealed a rock-cut rectangular kiln and, in 1964, a complete dump of tile debris and the partially disturbed stoke hole of a kiln were excavated. The tilery was situated

Plate 40 - One of the stamped tiles found by Ammon Wrigley in 1897-1907.

three miles east of the Roman fort at Slack, near Huddersfield (Grid Ref. SE 085174). It operated to provide building material for the two phases of reconstruction at Slack, c. AD 100 and 120. In addition to roofing and ridge tiles, *(tegula and imbrex)*, the tilery supplied the various items required in the construction of the hypocaust buildings, as well as the coarse- ware pottery that would be required by the occupants of the fort. The various excavations at Grimscar have produced a number of roofing tiles bearing the stamp COHIIIIBRE together with a quantity of coarse-ware pottery in colours and shapes that are well represented at the Roman fort at Slack.

Excavations at Slack have recovered in excess of eighty examples of roof tile bearing the stamp COHIIIIBRE. This is the stamp of the Fourth Cohort of the Breuci, a unit of five hundred auxiliary infantrymen. The cohort takes its name from the tribe who lived by the River Sava in modern Yugoslavia, from whose people it was raised.

Whilst no complete tile stamp has been recovered from Castleshaw, it is known that the tiles were manufactured at Grimescar. The date of the fort and later fortlet at Castleshaw compare with the two phases at Slack and it is obvious that the tilery, in addition to supplying Slack, also supplied Castleshaw.

Ammon Wrigley recovered two fragments of stamped tile during one of the periods he was working at Castleshaw. The first fragment had been cut into two parts and damaged with a spade. The stamp shows the letters CO and the outline of the rectangular frame around the letters. The second fragment shows the letters COH and the outline of the frame.

In 1907 Samuel Andrew found a piece of roofing tile near the hypocaust. The tile stamp was not well preserved and was first read as COHIIIBR. This is the stamp of the Third Cohort of the Bracaraugustani, an Iberian cohort from Bracara Augusta, the modern Braga in the north west of Portugal. Tile stamps of this cohort are known from the Roman forts at Manchester and Melandra. Later it was identified as a stamp of the Fourth Cohort of the Breuci. There is still some difference of opinion whether the stamp on the Castleshaw tile is COHIIIBR or COHIIIIBRE and doubt as to the existence of the final E. During the 1984-88 excavations, a further tile stamp was recovered from a spoil heap of the 1907 excavations. The fragment of tile shows IIIBRE outlined with a frame and was identified with the Fourth Cohort of the Breuci. It is not known whether the Breuci were ever stationed at Castleshaw, but they supplied it with tile and coarse ware pottery from the tilery eleven miles away.

Plate 41 - Stamped tile found by Andrew near the fortlet hypocaust in 1908.

Plate 42 - Stamped tile found in a Bruton spoil heap during the GMAU excavations of 1984-88

CHAPTER TEN

The Roman Name

Over the years, antiquarians have tried to discover the Roman name for the Agricolan auxiliary fort (Castleshaw 1).

In 1751 Thomas Percival, in his paper previously referred to, quoted, *Perhaps the names of Castlesteads, Castleshaw, Campfield, or some such other name, may yet remain to guide an antiquarian to the place, as the name of Castleshaw was the guide to me to find out the station, which I suppose to be Alunna.*

John Watson, in his paper, argued against Percival's suppositions. In discussing the Roman forts at Castleshaw the author concluded - *as the above has so many marks of a Roman station, the question is, by what name it was called. Ptolemy, Antonine, and the Notitia, are all silent about any station in these parts; but in the anonymous Ravenna, we have Mantio, Alunna, Camuludino, &c. the first of which, Mr Horsley, page 500, thinks must be designed for Manucium (Manchester), as in the Second Iter of Antonine. Alunna, he supposes, may be the same as Alone, in the Tenth Iter, fixed at Whitley Castle, in the South West corner of Northumberland; and Camulodunum, he says, both here, and in Ptolemy, must be the same with Camulodunum in the Second Iter above mentioned, which he has placed at Greetland in the parish of Halifax. But why must a station, within a few miles of the wall of Severus* (Hadrian's Wall), *be put between Manucium* (Manchester) *and Cambodunum* (Slack), *when yet the former is universally acknowledged to be Manchester in Lancashire, and the later to be only about 18 or 20 miles from the former.* It appears that Percival referred to Horsley's 'Britannia Romana' 1732 but incorrectly changed the name of Alunna to refer to Castleshaw.

Classical Sources

The main references available for Roman place names in Britain, and the distances between them, are the maps and route-books that have come down from classical sources and the standard work on Roman place names written in 1979 by A.L.F. Rivet and Colin Smith.

These are:

1) The Geography of Ptolemy. Ptolemy was an Egyptian geographer and mathematician who wrote during the reigns of Hadrian (A.D.117-138) and Antoninus Pius (A.D.138-161). He was the author of the most accurate and comprehensive geographical work of antiquity, although it contained serious errors, which are due to his having underrated the earth's circumference. The Geography takes the form of a list of the latitudes and longitudes of the known world. The information enabled a series of maps to be drawn and it is on the section covering the British Isles that we find a clue to the Roman name of Castleshaw. (see later discussion).

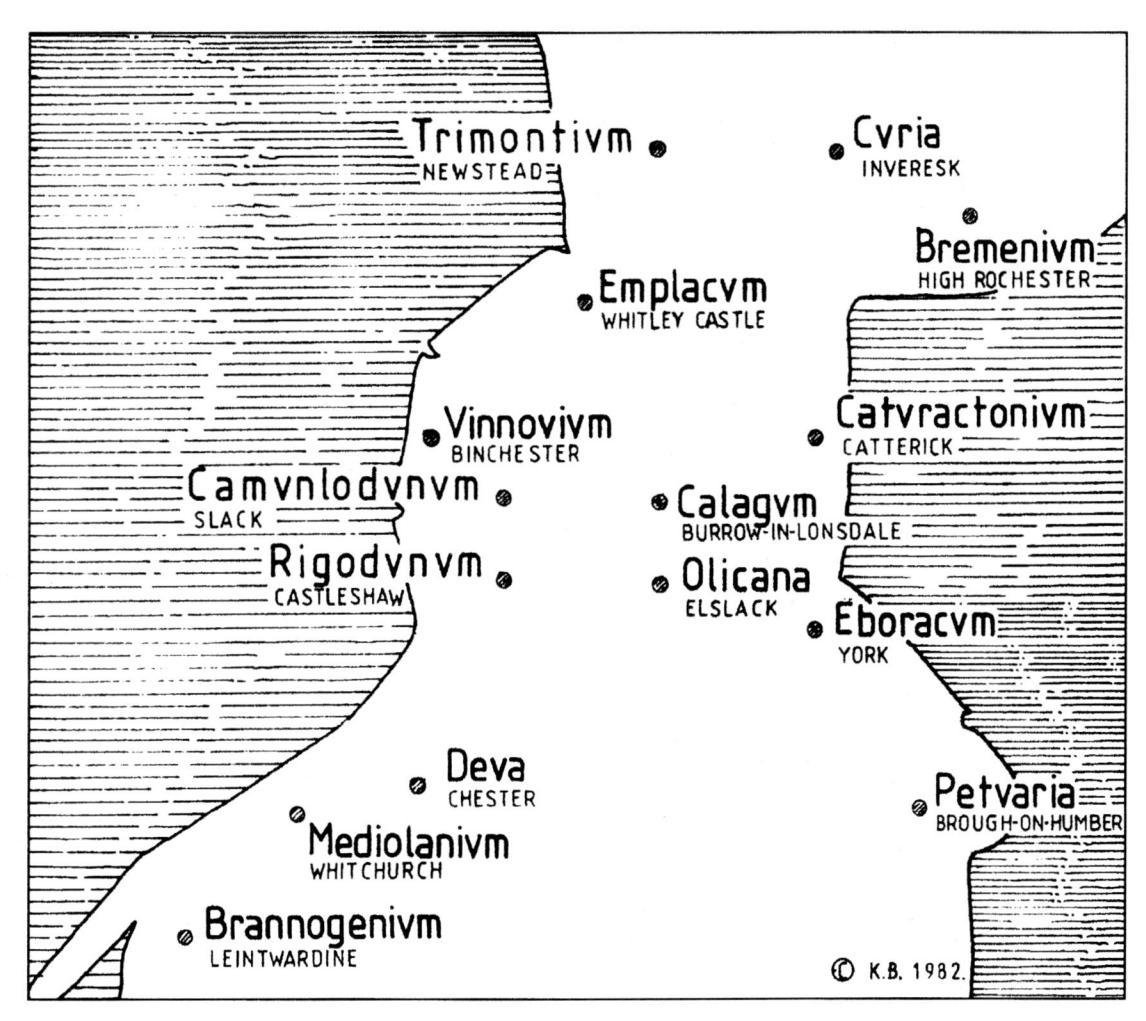

Figure 33 - The British Isles according to Ptolemy
Modern names are taken from 'The Place Names of Roman Britain' by Rivet and Smith. 1979

2) The Antonine Itinerary. This is generally considered to date from the end of the second or the beginning of the third century. It is a book of routes throughout the Roman Empire, probably prepared for the information of official travellers. It gave lists of places and staging-points, with distances along most of the major and some of the minor roads throughout the Empire.

3) The Peutinger Table. Named after Conrad Peutinger, the owner in the sixteenth century. It takes the form of a map and records places, routes and mileages. The surviving section dates from the thirteenth century and the Roman Empire is depicted upon a number of parchment sheets joined together in a long roll. Unfortunately, most of Britain was on the lost end sheet and the next sheet, which is greatly damaged. Only a small portion of the south and east coast of Britain, together with a few place names, is shown.

4) The Notitia Dignitatum. Dating from the fourth century, the British section gives the names of the forts in the frontier districts and those under the control of the Count of the Saxon Shore. It also listed the officials, officers, and military units of the Roman Empire with their respective stations.

The frontier district referred to was Hadrian's Wall. The Saxon Shore refers to the area of coast from Brancaster in Norfolk to Portchester in Hampshire. Along this stretch of coast is a chain of eleven Roman forts, dating mainly to the end of the third century A.D.

The forts were erected to protect the province against the Saxon sea-raiders who, at this period, were beginning to harry the coast of Britain, northern France and the Low Countries. The officer commanding the forts bore the title Comes Litoris Saxonici per Britannias – 'Count of the Saxon Shore of Britain'.

5) The Ravenna Cosmography. This is a seventh century compilation, based on various sources, probably including parts of The Antonine Itinerary and The Peutinger Table. It was the work of an anonymous cleric from Ravanna in Italy and is a list of the countries, towns and rivers of the known world. The list is corrupt in form. Though the compiler may have had a road map for Britain he chose to read names off the map in a random order within a given area, rather than a logical sequence along a road.

A Modern Study

6) The Place-Names of Roman Britain. This book written in 1979 by Rivet and Smith is the definitive work on its subject to-date. It examines the sources in great detail and in part two gives an alphabetical list of names, some 460 in all, each entry being divided into sections on the sources, derivations and modern identifications of the places, including map references.

Of the above sources, only Ptolemy gives any clue to a Roman name for Castleshaw. If the section of his map dealing with north-west England is enlarged, it immediately exposes the distortion that is known to exist. However, lying between Camulodunum (Slack, near Huddersfield) and Deva (Chester) is shown a site named Rigodunum. Rivet and Smith identify this site 'probably' as Castleshaw. More recent scholarly writings such as Graham Webster's 'Rome Against Caratacus', the 1994 Ordnance Survey Map of Roman Britain, and Hartley and Fitts 'The Brigantes', accept the Rigodunum identification for Castleshaw.

The Chester - York Roman road, its route passing through Saddleworth, is included in the Antonine Itinerary. The British section of the Itinerary is divided into fifteen sections; each starting with the word 'Item,' and the total distance from terminus to terminus is given at each site. The section covering Saddleworth is the ITER II, which starts at Birrens Roman fort (Blatobulgium) north of Carlisle and finishes at Richborough Port in Kent, a total distance of 492 English miles (792 kilometres). Given below is the section of the Itinerary covering the area between York and Chester.

Roman Name	Modern Name	Roman Miles	English Miles
Eburacum	York to		
Calcaria	Tadcaster to	VIIII	9.5
Cambodunum	Leeds to	XX	21
Manucio	Manchester to	XVIII *	19
Condate	Northwich to	XVIII	19
Deva, leg. XX Vict.	Chester	XX	21
* Originally perhaps XXVIII.			

The Roman mile, *milia passuum*, measures one thousand paces and corresponds to a distance of 1536metres compared to an English mile of 1609 metres. (1 Roman mile = 0.95 English miles)

No fort names are given between Leeds and Manchester, the area where the forts at Slack and Castleshaw lie. It is generally considered that the Antonine Itinerary dates from the end of the second century A.D. and, by this time both the forts had been abandoned, Slack in c.140A.D. and Castleshaw II in c.120A.D.

GLOSSARY

AGGER An artificial causeway on which the Roman road was built. It is sometimes just an earth bank or it may be carefully built up in layers of stony or other material. The actual road surface had a foundation of big stones upon which was laid gravel and small stones.

AGRICOLA Gnaeus Julius Agricola, the Roman governor of Britain from cAD77 - cAD84. During his time in office, both the Roman road and Castleshaw fort were built. The life of Agricola was well documented by his son-in-law Tacitus in his literary works of AD 97-98 *The Agricola and Germania.*

AMPHORA A large two-handled wine or oil jar.

ARMA The smaller front room occupied by eight men in a standard barrack building. This room was used for storing arms and equipment.

AUXILIARY Non-legionary soldiers recruited from the Roman provinces. After 25 years service and on discharge received citizenship for himself, his wife, and the children of that wife. The auxiliaries were composed of infantry and cavalry. The infantry unit, the cohors, had 1,000 men (millenary) or 500 (quingenary), the cavalry unit of the same size being the ala.

AUXILIARY FORT A permanently defended base for a single auxiliary unit of the Roman army. Originally built with turf ramparts and timber buildings, it was often rebuilt in stone. Normally rectangular in shape and 1 to 5 hectares in area, it was common in the first to third centuries AD.

BLANKET BOG An extensive peat bog existing as a consequence of high rainfall or humidity rather than of local water sources.

BOULDER-CLAY Clay containing many large stones and boulders, formed by deposition from melting glaciers and ice sheets.

BOREAL Designated or pertaining to a relatively warm dry climatic period in post-glacial Britain between the Preboreal and Atlantic periods, marked by the spread of hardwood forest.

BRONZE AGE The period, 1700BC-650BC, when weapons and tools were predominantly made of copper and its alloys.

CARBONIFEROUS The Carboniferous period, a system of coal bearing rocks dating from this time. They were laid down between 215 and 355 million years ago.

CENTURION	The commander of a century of men in the Roman army.
CENTURY	The cohorts were divided into centuries. The century seldom contained 100 men, it was usually 80 men commanded by a centurion.
COARSE WARE	The ordinary 'everyday' pottery of the Romans. Normally unglazed it came in a wide range of shapes, sizes and fabrics.
COHORT	The basic auxiliary unit of men. They were nominally 500 or 1000 men strong, with the smaller size predominating.
CROP-MARKS	Crops growing over buried wall foundations or roads will grow shorter than those growing over buried ditches or pits. The short crops tend to ripen early whereas the crops growing over deeper soil will be taller and ripen later thus showing as a different colour. Buried features can be revealed in extraordinary detail by these means when viewed from the air.
FABRICA	A Roman military workshop.
FOSSAE	The Latin name for ditches.
FLAVIAN	The period ruled by the Flavian dynasty; Vespasian - AD 69-79 Titus - AD 79-81 Domitian - AD 81-96
FORTLET	A small Roman military post usually square in shape and less than 0.5 hectares in area. It normally had a garrison of a small number of auxiliary troops. There was no standard layout for fortlets.
HADRIANIC	Belonging to the reign of the Emperor Hadrian, AD 117-138.
HORREA	The Latin name for granaries.
HYPOCAUST	A hollow space under a floor where hot air was circulated from a furnace to provide underfloor heating.
INTERVALLUM	A road passing around the internal perimeter of a fort or fortlet in the space between the rampart and buildings.
IRON AGE	A term used to describe the period when man exploited the mining of iron ore and the production and use of iron tools.
KINDER SCOUT GRIT	A coarse feldspathic sandstone.

LEGION	The primary unit of the Roman army. Recruited from Roman citizens, the legion was normally divided into 10 cohorts and each cohort into 6 centuries. The total strength was in excess of 5,000 men.
LEGIONARY FORTRESS	A large permanent base for a Roman legion. Either square or rectangular in shape, it usually occupied an area in excess of 20 hectares. Originally built of turf and timber it was rebuilt in stone from the second century onwards.
MESOLITHIC	A term used to describe the period between the old and new stone ages (Palaeolithic and Neolithic). Mesolithic man was semi-nomadic and survived by hunting and gathering.
MANSIO	A Roman posting station or inn. The term is often used for buildings set around a courtyard containing various rooms including baths and stables. The Imperial Post used them as an overnight stopping place.
MORTARIA	A Roman pottery mixing bowl.
NEOLITHIC	A term applied to the new stone age. Neolithic man was a farmer whose existence relied on the production of crops and the raising of domesticated animals.
PALAEO-ENVIRONMENT	The study of ancient environments through analysis of climatic change, ancient soils, fossil plant and ancient pollen remains.
PALAEOLITHIC	The emergence of man and the manufacture of the most ancient tools during the last Ice Age. Existed by hunting and gathering.
PAPILIO	The rear of the two rooms occupied by eight men in a standard barrack building. This room was used for sleeping.
PILAE	The pillars on which a hypocaust floor was supported.
PORTAE	The Latin name for gateways.
POST-HOLE	A hole made in the ground to receive a wooden post and sometimes packed with stones or clay for support.
PRAETENTURA	The area of a Roman fort which lay between the main gate and the main road crossing the fort *(via principalis)*.
PRAETORIUM	The house of the commanding officer of the garrison and his household. The arrangement was normally four ranges of rooms grouped around a central courtyard.

PRINCIPIA	The headquarters building of the fort. It was positioned centrally, opposite the junction of the two principal streets and facing towards the main front gate. This building was the administrative and religious focus of the fort.
PUNIC DITCH	A ditch form which had a steep, almost vertical outer scarp with a gentler inner slope. The profile tempted the attacker into the ditch who, when attempting to retreat, would be trapped by the near vertical scarp.
SAMIAN WARE	High-quality pottery used in Roman Britain. It was manufactured in Gaul during the first two centuries AD in a huge range of shapes, some of which were elaborately decorated. It was red in colour and had a glossy surface.
TRAJANIC	Belonging to the reign of the Emperor Trajan, AD 98-117.
VALLUM	A palisaded bank or rampart, formed of the earth dug up from the ditch or fosse around a Roman military camp. It is also used to describe the ditch and mounds which run to the south of Hadrian's Wall.
VESPASIAN	Roman emperor who reigned from AD69 until AD79.
VIA PRAETORIA	The road within a Roman fort that leads from the headquarters building *(principia)* to the main gate.
VIA PRICIPALIS	The main road passing through a Roman fort connecting two of the gates. Passing in front of the principal buildings it was joined by the *via praetoria*.
VIA SAGULARIS	The Latin name for the intervallum road.
VICUS	A civil settlement immediately outside a Roman fort administered by the Roman army.
YOREDALE SERIES	A cyclic sequence of thin beds of limestone and shale. They occur in the Tame Valley and can be seen where they have been exposed by the river.

BIBLIOGRAPHY

The following abbreviations have been used:

A.N.W.	Archaeology North West
Arch.	Journal of the Society of Antiquaries of London
Brit.	Britannia, published by the Society for the Promotion of Roman Studies
G.M.A.J.	The Greater Manchester Archaeological Journal
G.M.A.U.	The Greater Manchester Archaeological Unit
J.J.B.A.	Journal of the British Archaeological Association
S.A.T.	Saddleworth Archaeological Trust
S.H.S.	Publications of the Saddleworth Historical Society
T.L.A.C.A.S.	The Transactions of the Lancashire and Cheshire Antiquarian Society
Y.A.J.	The Journal of the Yorkshire Archaeological Society

Chapter 1 - The Setting

1)	Barnes B	1957	The Upper Tame Valley (unpublished thesis)	Manchester
2)	Bromehead C.E.N. *et al.*	1933	*The Geology of the Country around Holmfirth and Glossop*	H.M.S.O.
3)	Kidd L	1977	*Oldham's Natural History*	Oldham
4)	Kidd L. & Edwards W.F.	1997	*A Flora of Saddleworth*	Saddleworth
5)	Langridge B.	1996	*The Wild Flowers of Oldham*	Oldham
6)	Woodhead T.W.	1931	*Climate, Vegetation and Man in the Huddersfield District*	Huddersfield

Chapter 2 - Before the Romans

1)	Barnes B.	1982	*Man and the Changing Landscape*	Liverpool
2)	Bartley D. D.	1974	Pollen analytical evidence for prehistoric forest clearance in the upland area west of Rishworth.	New Phytol **74**
3)	Bradley R. J.	1978	*Prehistoric Settlement of Britain*	London
4)	Brayshay B.	1999	Some Palaeoenvironmental Evidence for Marginality in the Upper Mersey Basin	A.N.W. **3** (13)
5)	Brierley J.	1910	*Prehistoric Saddleworth*	Privately printed
6)	Evans J. G.	1978	*The Environment of Early Man in the British Isles*	London
7)	Stonehouse W.P.B.	2001	*The Prehistory of Saddleworth and Adjacent Areas*	S.A.T. **1**
8)	Watson G.G.	1952	*Early man in the Halifax District*	Halifax
9)	Wrigley A.	1911	*Saddleworth: Its Prehistoric Remains*	Oldham

Chapter 3 - Conquest and Occupation

1)	Frere S. S.	1967	*Britannia: a history of Roman Britain*	London
2)	Hartley B.R. & Fitts R. L.	1988	*The Brigantes*	Gloucester
3)	Higham N. J.	1986	*The Northern Counties to AD1000*	London
4)	Branigan K. (ed)	1980	*Rome and the Brigantes: the impact of Rome on Northern England*	Sheffield
5)	Salway P.	1981	*Roman Britain*	Oxford
6)	Wacher J.	1978	*Roman Britain*	London
7)	Webster G.	1978	*Boudica: the British revolt against Rome AD60*	London
8)	Webster G.	1980	*The Roman Invasion of Britain*	London
9)	Webster G.	1981	*Rome against Caratacus*	London

Chapter 4 - Roman Roads

1)	Bateson H.	1949	*A Centenary History of Oldham*	Oldham
2)	Barnes B.	1981	*Passage Through Time*	S.H.S.
3)	Booth K.	1987	*Castleshaw, Roads and Romans*	G.M.A.U.
4)	Bowman W.	1960	*England in Ashton-Under-Lyne*	Ashton-U-Lyne
5)	Butterworth E.	1856	*Historic Sketches of Oldham*	Oldham
6)	Butterworth J.	1817	*History of Oldham*	Oldham
7)	Butterworth J.	1828	*History of Rochdale and Saddleworth*	Oldham
8)	Bradbury J.	1871	*Saddleworth Sketches*	Oldham
9)	Chevallier R.	1967	*Roman Roads*	London
10)	Cleary A.S.E. (ed)	1996	*Roman Road, High Moor, Saddleworth*	Brit **27**
11)	Codrington T.	1919	*Roman Roads in Britain*	London
12)	Crump W.B.	1939	Saltways from the Cheshire Wiches	T.L.A.C.A.S. **54**
13)	Crump W.B.	1949	*Huddersfield highways down the ages*	Tolson Mem. Museum
14)	Earwaker J.P.	1880	*East Cheshire, Past and Present (2vols)*	London
15)	Haigh D. (ed)	1982	*Saddleworth Seven One Two*	Leeds
16)	Howcroft A.J.	1915	*Chapelry and Church of Saddleworth*	Oldham
17)	Johnston D.E.	1979	*Roman Roads in Britain*	Bourne End
18)	Jones G.D.B.	1971	The Roman road climbing Standedge	Brit **2**
19)	Margary I.D.	1967	*Roman Roads in Britain*	London
20)	Nevell M.D.	1992	*Tameside Before 1066*	Tameside
21)	Ormerod G.	1819	*The History of the County Palatine and City of Chester*	London
22)	Percival T.	1751	Observations upon the Roman stations in Lancashire and Cheshire	Royal Soc. of London. Philosophical Trans. **47**
23)	Richardson A.	1985	Some evidence of early Roman military activity on the south-west Pennine flank	J.B.B.A. **140**
24)	Watson Rev. J.	1760	Traces of another Roman Way in Lancashire	Oxford
25)	Watson Rev. J.	1770	Remains at Stalybridge	Oxford
26)	Whitaker Rev. J.	1773	*The History of Manchester*	London
27)	Wrigley A.	1912	*Songs of a Moorland Parish*	Uppermill
28)	Watkin W.T.	1883	*Roman Lancashire*	Liverpool
29)	Watkin W.T.	1886	*Roman Cheshire*	Liverpool
30)	Whittaker G.H.	1926	*Hill Tops in Four Shires*	Stalybridge
31)	Wilson D.R. (ed)	1974	Excavations in Thurston Clough	Brit **5**
32)	Wilson D.R. (ed)	1974	Excavations in Oldgate Clough	Brit **5**
33)	Goodburn R. (ed)	1976	Excavations at Causeway Sett	Brit **7**
34)	Goodburn R. (ed)	1978	Geophysical survey to locate link road to west gate of fort	Brit **9**

Chapter 5 - The Roman Forts

1)	Andrew S.	1898	The Roman camp at Castleshaw and the antiquities of the Saddleworth district	T.L.A.C.A.S. **16**
2)	Andrew S.	1907	Recent finds at Castleshaw	T.L.A.C.A.S. **25**
3)	Booth K.	1972	The Roman forts at Castleshaw	Bull. S.H.S. **2** (pt.3)
4)	Booth K.	1983	The Pennines under Rome	Pennine Mag. **4** No 6
5)	Booth K.	1984	The Roman forts at Castleshaw	Hadrianic Soc. Bull. **2**
6)	Bruton F.A.	1908	Excavation of the Roman forts at Castleshaw	Y.A.J. **20**
7)	Bruton F.A.	1908	*Excavation of the Roman forts at Castleshaw 1st Interim Report*	Manchester
8)	Bruton F.A.	1911	*Excavation of the Roman forts at Castleshaw 2nd Interim Report*	Manchester
9)	Buckley G.F.	1898	Explorations at Castleshaw	T.L.A.C.A.S. **16**
10)	Percival T.	1751	Observations upon the Roman stations in Lancashire and Cheshire	Royal Soc. of London. Philosophical Trans. **47**
11)	Petch J.A.	1961	The Roman forts at Castleshaw: excavations 1957-61	T.L.A.C.A.S. **71**
12)	Richmond I.A.	1925	The sequence and purpose of the Roman forts at Castleshaw	T.L.A.C.A.S. **40**

13)	Richmond I.A.	1925	*Huddersfield in Roman times*	Huddersfield
14)	Rosser C.E.P.	1958	Interim report on excavations at Castleshaw	T.L.A.C.A.S. **67**
15)	Start D.R.	1985	Survey and conservation work at Castleshaw Roman forts	G.M.A.J. **1**
16)	Start D.R. *et al.*	1986	Excavation and conservation at Castleshaw Roman forts	G.M.A.J. **2**
17)	Start D.R. *et al.*	1987 1988	Excavation and conservation at Castleshaw Roman forts	G.M.A.J. **3**
18)	Thompson F.H.	1974	The Roman forts at Castleshaw, Yorkshire Excavations 1957-64	T.L.A.C.A.S. **77**
19)	Walker J. (ed)	1989	*Castleshaw-The Archaeology of a Roman Fortlet*	G.M.A.U.
20)	Watson Rev. J.	1766	Some account of a Roman station lately discovered on the borders of Yorkshire	Archaeologia **1**
21)	Whitaker Rev. J.	1771	*The History of Manchester*	London
22)	Wrigley A.	1912	The first excavations of the Roman camp at Castleshaw in *Songs of a Moorland Parish*	Uppermill

Chapter 6 - Outside the Forts

1)	Brayshay B.	1998	Some Palaeoenvironmental Evidence for Marginality in the Upper Mersey Basin	A.N.W. **3** (13)
2)	Cracknell D.G.	1964	*Law Students Companion No 4. Roman Law*	London
3)	Start D.R.	1987	A possible Roman signal station on Standedge	G.M.A.U. **3**
4)	Redhead N.	1996	Daycroft Field, Castleshaw	Bull. S.H.S. **26** (pt 1)
5)	Redhead N.	1996	Castleshaw Evaluation Stage 2 - further investigations of extra-mural activity at an upland Roman military site	Bull. S.H.S. **27** (pt 1)
6)	Redhead N.	1998	Edge of Empire, extra-mural settlement in a marginal context, Roman Castleshaw	A.N.W. **3** (13)

Chapter 7 - The Finds

1)	Buckley G.F.	1898	Explorations at Castleshaw	T.L.A.C.A.S. **16**
2)	Oldham Museum		Record of finds from Wrigley's excavations	1897-1907
3)	Oldham Museum		Record of finds from G.M.A.U. excavations	1984-1988
4)	Manchester Museum		Record of finds from Bruton's excavations	1908-1909
5)	Manchester Museum		Record of finds from Thompson's excavations	1957-1964
6)	Watson Rev. J.	1766	Some account of a Roman station lately discovered on the borders of Yorkshire	Archaeologia **1**
7)	Wrigley A.	1912	The first excavations of the Roman camp at Castleshaw in *Songs of a Moorland Parish*	Uppermill
8)	Teasdill G.	1961	*Coin finds of the Huddersfield district*	Huddersfield

Chapter 8 - The Roman coins from Saddleworth

1)	Booth K.	1983	The Roman coins of Saddleworth	Bull. S.H.S. **13** (pt 1)
2)	Carpenter F.	1981	Some Roman coins from the Oldham and Saddleworth areas	Bull. S.H.S. **11** (pt 4)
3)	Redhead N.	1989	Stamped Tiles in Walker 1989	G.M.A.U.
4)	Shotter D.C.A.	1990	*Roman coins from North-West England*	Lancaster
5)	Shotter D.C.A.	1993	Roman coins from Castleshaw	Manchester Arch. Bull. **8**
6)	Shotter D.C.A.	2000	*Roman coins from North-West England*	Lancaster
7)	Teasdill G.	1961	*Coin finds of the Huddersfield district*	Huddersfield
8)	Walker J. (ed)	1989	*Castleshaw - The Archaeology of a Roman Fortlet*	G.M.A.U.
8)	Webster P.V.	1989	The Samian Pottery in Walker 1989	G.M.A.U.

Chapter 9 - The Tile Stamps from Castleshaw

1)	Booth K.	1980	The Stamped Tiles from Castleshaw	Bull. S.H.S. **10** (pt 1)
2)	Brodribb G.	1987	*Roman Brick and Tile*	Gloucester
3)	Collingwood R.G. & Wright R.P.	1992	*The Roman Inscriptions of Britain Vol. 2 Fascicule 4*	Stroud
4)	Hassall M.	1979	Military Tile-Stamps from Britain in *Roman Brick and Tile ed. A. McWhirr*	B.A.R. Inter. Series **68**
5)	Holder P.A.	1982	*The Roman Army in Britain*	London
6)	Purdy J.G. & Manby T.G.	1973	Excavations at the Roman Tilery at Grimscar, Huddersfield	Y.A.J. **45**
7)	Richmond I.A.	1925	*Huddersfield in Roman Times*	Huddersfield

Chapter 10 - The Roman Name

1)	Booth K.	1983	The Roman name of the Agricolan fort at Castleshaw	Bull. S.H.S. **13** (pt 4)
2)	Goodburn R. & Bartholomew P.	1976	*Aspects of the Notitia Dignitatum*	B.A.R. Supp. Series 15
3)	Ordnance Survey	1978	*Map of Roman Britain-Fourth Edition*	Southampton
4)	Ordnance Survey	1994	*Map of Roman Britain*	Southampton
5)	Rivet A.L.F.	1970	The British Section of the Ravenna Cosmography	Archaeologia 93
6)	Rivet A.L.F. & Smith C.	1979	*The Place Names of Roman Britain*	London